THE FATHER OF THE
LITTLE FLOWER

"For God hath made the father honourable to the children . . ."
—Ecclesiasticus 3:3

Louis Martin—1823-1894

THE FATHER
OF THE
LITTLE FLOWER

LOUIS MARTIN
1823-1894

By

Celine Martin

(Sister Genevieve of the Holy Face)

Translated from the French by
Fr. Michael Collins, S.M.A.

THE SISTER OF ST. THÉRÈSE
TELLS US ABOUT HER FATHER

TAN BOOKS AND PUBLISHERS, INC.
Rockford, Illinois 61105

Nihil Obstat: Edward Gallen
                    Censor Deputatus

Imprimi Potest: ✛ John Charles [McQuaid]
                    Archbishop of Dublin
                    Primate of Ireland
                    Dublin, March 7, 1955

First published in 1955—presumably by M. H. Gill and Son, Ltd., Dublin—as well as by The Newman Press, Westminster, Maryland, in 1955. Reprinted in 2005 by TAN Books and Publishers, Inc. by permission of the Office Central de Lisieux.

ISBN 0-89555-812-2

Photo on cover and on frontispiece: Louis Martin.

Anyone who has received favors through the intercession of Louis and/or Zélie Martin may make them known to the Carmel of Lisieux, 37 rue du Carmel, 14100 Lisieux, France, or to the Postulator General of the Discalced Carmelites, Corso d'Italia 38, 00198 Roma, Italy.

Printed and bound in the United States of America.

TAN BOOKS AND PUBLISHERS, INC.
P.O. Box 424
Rockford, Illinois 61105
2005

"To the love of God, to the spirit of faith and hope was joined in my father's character an immense charity towards his neighbor. That was his outstanding virtue."

—*Celine Martin*

"He certainly had insurmountable courage, prompt decision, endurance and energy. He was a true son of an army officer."

—*Celine Martin*

Monsieur Martin was "so courageous! He was afraid of nothing. . . ."

—*A household servant of the Martin family*

"His charity was most admirable; he never expressed an unkind judgment in regard to anyone, and always found an excuse for the wrong-doing of a neighbour."

—*Friends of Louis Martin in Alençon*

Letter of His Excellency, Msgr. Picaud, Bishop of Bayeux and Lisieux, to the Reverend Mother Prioress of the Carmel of Lisieux:

Bayeux, July 29, 1953.

Reverend Mother and dear Daughter in Christ,

You know so well the profound esteem which I hold for the venerable parents of St. Thérèse of the Child Jesus, that you cannot doubt of my approval of the project to publish a booklet on the *moral portrait of M. Martin.*

I have always emphasized to the living sisters of the dear saint that they should carefully collect all the memories, concerning not only their glorious little sister, but also their incomparable father and mother.

All I can do then is heartily to encourage Sister Geneviève of the Holy Face, the only remaining witness of that privileged family to sketch for us the faithful portrait of M. Martin, to whom she was an angel of consolation in his suffering.

And let me add also that it is very opportune to have this publication at present in order to rectify certain regrettable errors which have been advanced by poorly-informed writers.

It is a duty to restore the truth with the help of authentic documents which correct any biased commentaries, and thus render to the magnificent personality of the father of St. Thérèse his incontestable greatness both psychological and supernatural.

Nor should it be forgotten that in proclaiming the Heroicity of the Virtues of St. Thérèse of the Child Jesus His Holiness, Benedict XV, was pleased to praise her father who, as a " *true model of Christian parents*, did not hide the noble pride he felt in consecrating to God in the Religious Life all his descendants." (Discourse, August 14, 1921).

Examples such as that are more needed now than ever before to restore Christian families and through them our decadent modern society.

Accept, Reverend Mother and dear Daughter in Christ, my paternal benediction with best wishes for the beneficial results of this enterprise.

François-Marie,
Bishop of Bayeux and Lisieux.

To the Reverend Mother Françoise Thérèse of the Child Jesus and of the Holy Face, Prioress of the Carmel of Lisieux:

J.M.J.T.

Reverend Mother,

As the publication of the *Letters* of our dear mother led to an appreciation of her by the public, you have asked me to make known our venerable father also, as he really was, in recollecting my memories of four score years. To be sure, the essentials are found in *The Story of a Family*. The author had at his disposal, and scrupulously utilized, all the written and oral documentation given by Mother Agnes and myself. That book can be relied upon absolutely.

However, in order to accede to your wishes I have tried to state my personal recollections in regard to my father. To write a special biography would be useless, since it is already given in *The Story of a Family*. I have therefore grouped together a certain number of characteristics which will outline the moral portrait, so to say, of our father.

I submit this writing to you, Reverend Mother, in the same spirit of simplicity with which it was written. I can assure you that the desire for truth alone is what has urged and guided me in this endeavour. From these statements, as well as from *The Story of a Family* and the *Letters* of my mother, one can judge of the value of some statements that may be heard at Alençon and at Lisieux in regard to our parents, our family life, and our relations with other persons in former days.

Many experiences have proved to me that frequently inaccuracies and strange imaginings become blended in. These erroneous remarks pass from person to person and finally cover up the truth entirely, just as the successive layers of sediment conceal the sea-shell and the beauty of the mother-of-pearl.

I wish also to add, Reverend Mother, with regard to the use of the word " saint," sometimes attributed to my parents, or quoted by other witnesses of their virtues, that this expression has only a strictly private value.

> Sister Geneviève of the Holy Face
> and of St. Teresa.
>
> Carmel of Lisieux, September 30, 1952.
>
> *Feast of St. Thérèse of the Child Jesus.*

CONTENTS

THE FATHER
OF THE
LITTLE FLOWER

*"The good God gave me a father
and mother more worthy of Heaven
than of earth."*
—St. Thérèse of the Child Jesus
Letter 261

MORAL PORTRAIT OF MY FATHER

My father, Louis Martin, was born at Bordeaux on August 22, 1823. He was the son of a French army officer stationed at that time in the city, but originally from Normandy. He was privately baptized, but the Baptismal Ceremonies were retarded on account of the absence of Captain Martin, who was then engaged in a military expedition in Spain, from which he returned decorated with the Cross of Knight of the Royal and Military Order of St. Louis. At his Baptism the holy Archbishop of Bordeaux, Monsignor d'Ariau, happened to meet the baptismal group in the Church of St. Eulalie. Graciously he came over to the baby, blessed him, and said to the happy parents: "*Congratulations! That child is a predestined one.*"

We know from *The Story of a Family* and the Preface of *The Story of a Soul,* that the aspirations of the young Louis turned towards the Religious life. About the age of twenty he tried to enter the Religious Order of the Great St. Bernard (Alps). As he could not be admitted without a knowledge of Latin, he studied it privately for some time. (The only foreign language he knew was German).

Turning rather late in life to the establishing of a home, on July 13, 1858, he married

Zélie Guérin, who was directing an enterprise of lace-making (Point d'Alençon). She was the daughter of a soldier of Napoleon, who on retiring had joined the Constabulary. Madame Martin died prematurely after having become the mother of nine children, of whom four went to Heaven while still young.

It was then that he came with us, his five daughters, to reside at Lisieux, where our maternal uncle, M. Isidore Guérin, had a pharmacy. We lived in the property known as Les Buissonnets, a three-storey house with a lawn and a garden. The top storey was called the Belvedere, which will be mentioned a number of times in this narrative.

PIETY—LOVE OF GOD

As a young man, my father stayed with his parents at Alençon, in the suburbs of St. Pierre de Monsort, where they were then living. While there he made several excursions to Brittany, whence he returned gaily dressed in Breton costume. Other years he travelled as far as the Swiss mountains.

A lady who knew the family at that time but had lost sight of them through the years wrote fifty-six years later at the first publication of *The Story of a Soul:* [1]

---

[1] Sister St. Francis de Sales Desroziers, Religious of Our Lady of Charity, Caen. Letter of April, 1899.

" Reading this (*The Story of a Soul*) has left me enraptured, and all the more so as it recalls a highly respected family, which was esteemed and loved for a long time at Alençon.

" The grandmother, Madame Martin, lived next door to us; her son, Louis Martin, was the friend of my brothers. When he returned from Mount St. Bernard, I can distinctly recall him, and hear his happy mother exclaiming: ' Ah! my Louis, my dearest Louis, he is a real pearl! ' She was right; and my brothers used to say to us : " Louis Martin is a saint.' "

Some time afterwards my father opened a watch and jewelry shop in the Monsort district, at 23 Pont-Neuf Street; his parents went to live with him. Besides, he purchased outside the town a small property called the Pavilion, with a hexagonal tower at the corner of a garden, where he used to retire to read quietly and to pray, having kept his taste for the life of the cloister. He himself had inscribed on the inside walls sentences such as: " *God sees me*," " *Eternity is drawing near.*" The austerity of the place so frightened a worldly lady that she ran away in fear, as our eldest sister, Marie, used to tell us with amusement.

However, that attraction for silence and solitude did not prevent his piety from being broad and sympathetic. It was at the same time

tender, but without affectation. In the garden
of the Pavilion he had placed a statue of the
Blessed Virgin, which was to become later an
object of veneration for the whole family, and
to smile on Thérèse as a child.

In his youth his virtue had withdrawn him
from the seductions of the world. Our mother
gives an example of it to her brother, who
was then a medical student in Paris.

> "My dear Brother, I am very anxious
> about you. My husband frequently repeats
> his sad forebodings of your dangers. He
> knows Paris, and he tells me that you will
> be exposed to dangers; he fears you will
> not resist the temptations, for you are not
> devout enough. He relates what he himself
> endured, and that it required courage
> on his part to overcome those struggles
> victoriously. If you only knew what trials
> he had to undergo. . . I beg you, my dear
> Isidore, imitate him, mind your prayers,
> and you will not be carried along by the
> torrent." [1]

* * *

Our father went daily to Mass, and also to
Holy Communion as often as the custom of
the time allowed. Accompanied by our mother

[1] January 1, 1863.

he left the house early, so much so that the neighbours used to say at the sound of the closing of the door: " That is the holy Martin couple going to Mass, let us sleep some more! " While they lived at St. Blaise Street, where Thérèse was born, it was to Notre Dame (Our Lady's, Alençon) that they went. The church has a marvellous outside porch, a fact which lent itself to a popular but rather irreverent local saying:

In such a way the Church was made,
    That to prepare the choicest spot
Wherein to place Our Lord, they said,
    Outside the door would be His lot!

But for these virtuous parents it was not in the outside porch of their lives that God had His abode, but in the centre of their hearts all devoted to His service. Always attentive to the church services, our parents were perfect models of parochial life.[1] At Lisieux it was most often at the Cathedral that my father assisted at Mass. The days on which he went to Holy Communion he generally remained silent on his return journey. " I like to continue

---

[1] With regard to the parish of St. James, which was ours at Lisieux, I must say that, on account of the impossibility of having seats together in that church, we used to prefer going to the Cathedral. That parish was less crowded, and was nearer to Les Buissonnets. But we were always on good terms with all the clergy of the town.

my conversation with Our Lord," he used to say to us.

Every afternoon he used to pay a visit to the Blessed Sacrament, and whenever there was a " Corpus Christi " Procession he never missed being directly behind the canopy. On no account would he have stayed away, even when the sun was very hot—something he minded very much as obviously he always had his head uncovered. This devotion to Our Lord in the Tabernacle manifested itself also by his exemplary fidelity to Nocturnal Adoration. He was one of the first to arrive at the appointed hour; and when free to choose he selected the most inconvenient hours, and gladly changed with someone else if a more favourable hour fell to his lot. At Lisieux, where this pious practice had not been established, he persuaded our uncle, M. Guérin, who belonged to the Board of Consultors of the Cathedral, to introduce it there.

Many times at Alençon, where it was the custom, he was seen with a lighted candle accompanying the priest carrying Viaticum to a sick person. I say it was the custom, because this pious custom was approved of, but very few men went as far as that. In the same way I noticed that in passing a church he always raised his hat, and this irrespective of the company with whom he was walking. His reverence for the House of God manifested itself on another occasion by a striking act of generosity. In 1888 he spontaneously offered the sum of 10,000 francs (at that time £400, or 2,000 dollars) which was required to purchase a new High-Altar for the Lisieux Cathedral.

FAITH—HOPE IN GOD

What can one say in regard to the spirit of faith, and the invincible hope of our father: " God is everything," " God above all! " The motto of St. Ignatius also was dear to him: " All for the greater glory of God! "

Often in the Belvedere of Les Buissonnets one of us would find him plunged in deep meditation, looking out into the distance with an expression of heavenly happiness. And many times we heard him murmuring: " *Ego ero merces tua magna nimis.*" His soul was filled with this thought; it was overflowing with it. Then, stressing each syllable he would repeat it in translation : " I am thy reward exceeding great." [1] We had been so struck by this, that this text, which he had loved so much, was printed at the heading of his mortuary card.

Everything which referred to Our Lord touched him deeply. One Christmas Day

---

[1] *Gen.* xv. 1.

towards the end of his life he said to Sister
Agnes at the Carmel parlour: "A little Child!
a Babe! Ah! how can a person not be drawn
to love the good God who so annihilated
Himself! A babe is so lovely!" He had also
a great devotion to the Five Wounds. Frequently
I heard him speaking with our mother about
Heaven, and Eternity. He liked to repeat the
poem of Lamartine:

"Man! Time is nothing for an immortal being.
Unfortunate he who tries to store it up.
Foolish he who weeps for it.
Time is your sailing-ship and not your home."

Later on this figure of a ship was to be
recalled by Thérèse. Spiritual reading nourished
these thoughts. At the Pavilion of Alençon,
as in the Belvedere of Lisieux, there were only
books dealing with the things of faith. It is
through our father, to whom Sister Agnes had
loaned it, that Thérèse made the acquaintance
of the book of Abbé Arminjon: *The End of the
Present World, and the Mysteries of the Life to Come*
a work which did her so much good.

Our father also used to make *Closed Retreats*.
At the Trappist Monastery of Soligny they have
on record the dates of one of his stays there.
He also liked to make pilgrimages, to which
he used to add some form of penance. Walking-

stick in hand, he would start out fasting for Our Lady's of Seez, or some nearer shrine around Alençon. He visited Chartres also several times. His object was to implore some special grace, the cure of one of his sick children, or aid for France in some national crisis or calamity.

Human respect did not affect him. On the contrary, he took a kind of pride in proclaiming his religious opinions. Once a local pilgrimage returning from Lourdes encountered in the station at Alençon a crowd which had come to jeer at them. Assuming the cause of the pilgrims he went to the head of the frightened group and, wearing a large carved wood rosary round his neck, he passed boldly through the midst of the crowd which stopped jeering and quickly dispersed.

On another occasion as he was passing in the Procession of the Blessed Sacrament he quickly tipped off the hat of a sneering individual who through bravado would not take it off when the Monstrance was borne along. Moreover the enemies of religion always treated him with respect, although more than once he gave them lessons by his conduct. Again he could not endure to see Mass-servers careless and forgetful of their duties. I was surprised one day to see him get up at the Consecration of the Mass and go up himself to ring the hand-bell,

which happened to be placed near the congregation, when the boys neglected to do so.

He did not believe in taking part in
entertainments of hypnotism or spiritualism.
One evening a friendly group wished to experiment with " turning tables " and " making
them talk." He quietly refused to co-operate.
While the others were joining hands around, he
prayed in his heart : " Lord, if the devil has
anything to do with this, do not allow the table
to turn." As a matter of fact they could not
budge it, a failure which the others attributed
to him.

The laws of fasting and abstinence were
strictly observed by him, even when nominal
Catholics were enjoying his hospitality. Our
Mother writes to her brother, May 16, 1864:

" You say that our aunt from Paris is
coming this week. We are all delighted at
that news and are anticipating it in advance.

" You tell me she will spend only one day
with us (at Alençon). I wish she would
stay longer. But I should be so glad if you
could persuade her not to come until the
week after next. This is the reason: next
week Wednesday, Friday and Saturday are
Ember Days. You know that Louis is a
strict observer of the Commandments of
the Church. He would not wish at any cost
to eat meat, or not to fast on those days;

and I doubt very much if our aunt would care to follow the law.

"When M. D. came during Lent, you would not believe how embarrassed we felt. Louis was the only one fasting, since I am dispensed for the time being. He had to watch us eating nice things while he was taking just his light collation. And we had to keep the abstinence."

Especially noticeable was our father's solicitude in regard to keeping Sunday holy. The Lord's Day was sacred for him, so much so that his friends considered that he sometimes exaggerated its observance. They insisted that he should open his jewelry shop, at least by a back-door, pointing out that he was losing opportunities to do good business, for on the other side of the street was a large novelty department-store that drew crowds on holidays. For the most part these crowds were country people who came into Alençon to buy presents for their festivities on the occasion of baptisms, marriages, New Year's Day, etc. But his friends could not prevail on him to do so. Though for others the temptation would have been insurmountable, he did not succumb to it.

For the same reason he did not buy anything on Sunday. Once having noticed for sale on the passing cart of a hawker a grindstone that he wanted, he asked the man to hold it for him until the following day. We ourselves followed the same principle at home. On Sundays we had stale bread that had to be bought the preceding day. And it was a rare occasion for us to undertake a journey on Sunday which might require another person to work.

In a letter addressed to her sister-in-law, Madame Guérin, September 29, 1875, our mother declares:

> "Very often I admire the strictness of Louis, and I say to myself: 'There's a man who never tried to amass a fortune.' When he was starting in business, his confessor suggested to him—so he told me—to open his jewelry store on Sundays until noon. But Louis never wanted to use that permission preferring rather to lose business. In spite of that he has become rich. I can attribute his comfortable financial position to no other cause than a special blessing of God, a result of his faithful observance of Sunday."

But God goes still further in His promises when He proclaims solemnly: *If thou turn away thy foot from the Sabbath, from doing thy own will in my holy day, and call the Sabbath delightful . . . then . . . I will lift thee up above the high places of the earth. . . For the mouth of the Lord hath spoken it.*[1]

---

[1] *Isaias* lviii. 13, 14.

With regard to his veneration for the priesthood, I affirmed in my deposition of the Apostolic Process for the canonization of my saintly little sister how much I was edified in seeing Papa saluting all priests whom he met:

> " His respect for priests was so great that I never saw anything like it. I remember when I was a little child I imagined from what I had heard that priests were like gods; I was so accustomed to have them placed above the common level."

I never heard him express a criticism of the clergy, nor find fault with a sermon. He listened with a devout respect to the word of God, without considering the quality of the instrument which transmitted it.

His regular confessor at Lisieux was Abbé Lepelletier, an assistant-priest at the Cathedral, and he gladly consulted the Rev. Father Pichon, S.J., whom he liked to call the Spiritual Director of the whole Martin family. That eminent Religious was besides a compatriot, having been born at Carrouges (Orne).

On reading over these lines written as my pen runs on, and as the stream of memory carries me along, I notice that I frequently employ the words " never " and " always." That is because our father had in all moods and tenses, so to say, a military uprightness. His virtues never swerved; they followed tracks firmly fixed in the ground without any possibility of being upset one way or the other.

SPIRIT OF ZEAL

Our parents were greatly interested in the salvation of souls. They prayed and had prayers said for sinners; especially when in the neighbourhood any one of them was in danger of death, they tried to arrange that he should receive the Last Sacraments. While Pauline was a boarding pupil at the Visitation Convent at Le Mans, our mother wrote on May 14, 1876:

> " I recommend to your prayers, and especially to those of your aunt, a poor man who is dying. He has not gone to Confession for forty years. Your father is doing all he can to persuade him to be converted."

The Poor Clares of Alençon, and later the Carmel of Lisieux, were asked to lend their spiritual assistance. At that time there were not so many charitable associations or specialized movements as there are to-day. But our father was generally a member of those that existed, such as the Catholic Circle of Alençon, and the Conference of St. Vincent de Paul, of which he was an active member.   Later on he was inscribed on the list of the Founders of the Parish Association of St. James at Lisieux, for us the best known work of apostolic zeal to which each year our parents gave a very substantial sum.

Into their prayers entered the great intentions of the Church and of the Holy Father.   It was with sadness that we often heard at home of the misfortunes of the Church, of the moral imprisonment of the Roman Pontiff, of the rumblings of persecution in France and in the whole world.   I must stress, however, that above all personal prayers our parents had recourse to the Holy Sacrifice of the Mass, and that they were particularly anxious to have Masses celebrated for the faithful departed.

It will be seen further on how this solicitude for his neighbours' welfare continued on in our father's mind even in the suffering of his own illness.   It is on account of their zeal for souls that my parents desired so much to have a missionary son and consecrated daughters. Through devotion for the Apostle of the Indies our father liked to sign himself " Xavier," although that name is not among those he received in Baptism.   Our parents might easily have confined their interests to their own family circle, and have lived just for the enjoyment of their own home; but instead they widened our horizons and made us think of others. Thus it was our father who spoke to Thérèse of the impenitent and condemned Pranzini who owes his salvation to her. One has only to read the letters of our mother to verify how much she had the spirit of zeal in her soul.

COURAGE AND CHARITY TO HIS NEIGHBOURS

To the love of God, to the spirit of faith and of hope was joined in my father's character an immense charity towards his neighbour. That was his outstanding virtue. If the fire-alarm bell rang at night he got up immediately to rush wherever the danger was greatest. Once when I was a day-boarder at the Benedictine Abbey, I was speaking of this to my companions, when one of them exclaimed: " At our home, it is just the opposite. At the sound of the alarm bell Papa hides under the blankets." That astonished me.

That well-known bravery of his sometimes made us anxious when we did not see him returning at the usual time. We used to be afraid that perhaps in separating persons who were fighting he might have got a dangerous blow himself; or that he might have gone to

the rescue of some drowning person, for he
was a very good swimmer, and he would not
have hesitated to risk his own life to save that
of another. In his youth he had rescued several
from drowning. One case in particular was
quite dramatic; he almost lost his own life
when his struggling companion clutched him
around the neck and seriously obstructed all
his movements.

I have always thought that in his desire for
the religious life, his choice of the Great
St. Bernard, with its heights and solitude
beyond the noise of the cities, was not un-
connected with his attraction for the danger
connected with rushing to the rescue of travellers
in distress on the glaciers of the Alps. In the
same way I have often said to myself, when
hearing of the various modern organisations
for youth: if our father was so happy in other
days to be in a " Boys' Military Club," how he
would have enjoyed belonging to the Scouts
if they had existed at that time. To camp out
anywhere in the open would have been his
delight. He certainly had insurmountable
courage, prompt decision, endurance and energy.
He was a true son of an Army Officer.

This paragraph from one of my mother's
letters, referring to the military occupation
of Alençon by the Prussians in November, 1870,
is quite to the point:

> " It is still quite possible that the men of
> forty to fifty years of age will be conscripted;
> I almost expect it. My husband is not in
> the least troubled by that. He would not
> claim exemption, and he often says that if
> he were free he would soon be among the
> volunteers."

His extraordinary coolness had been noticed
by the household servants. One of the maids
at Les Buissonnets, writing to Carmel, recalls
the fact thus:[1]

> " M. Martin was above all a saint, and so
> courageous! He was afraid of nothing. . ."

The truth is that wherever there was danger
at any point he rushed to that spot, as I have
already said. When we were living at Alençon,
one night during " Nocturnal Adoration " at
Notre Dame he found the men's dormitory on
fire. An over-heated stove had started the
fire. It was an occasion for him to show all his
ingenuity and interest. He tried to save all
he could by throwing mattresses, etc., out
of the windows. My mother's letters refer to
the incident.

One morning a fire was raging in the interior
of a hovel opposite Les Buissonnets. He ran
to the help of the poor inmate, an elderly

---

[1] Mme. Felicité Saffray.

Irishwoman, who was all alone in the wretched cabin, and put out the flames. In such cases he preferred to be alone, and stopped others from shouting "Fire!" lest dishonest persons should come to steal. The poor woman raised her arms to Heaven, begging God in her native tongue to pour down His blessings on her rescuer. I myself was a witness of that scene.

As for the details of the following incident, I have heard my father tell it. His presence of mind was manifested in it. This is what happened. Having gone fishing near Lisieux he found himself at close quarters with an enraged bull which he suddenly discovered breaking to bits his box of fishing tackle a little distance away. To snatch up his fish-lines and to run for his life was the work of an instant. But the beast rushed after him so closely that undoubtedly he would have been knocked to the ground except for a move as bold as it was quick. From a distance he kept turning towards the bull and threatening the creature with his pile of fishing-rods, which made it draw back. Profiting by the territory gained, Father ran ahead, renewing the same tactics over and over again until at last he reached the fence of the pasture.

My father used to end his story with these words: "Thank God with me, children. Without His protection you might never again have seen me alive." This shows he realized his extreme danger. In this circumstance Father had by his remarkable presence of mind saved his own life. He would not have hesitated to risk it for a stranger caught in the same critical situation.

* * *

This natural bravery changed to charity in other fields of activity, as circumstances occurred. At Alençon I was present on several occasions when my mother shared with him the honour and merit of good works. I remember a poor tramp whom they found worn out by the roadside. They brought him to our house, gave him plenty of nourishing food, then got better clothes and boots for him. While he was trying these on, his face beamed with such a happy look that after all these years— I was then only about seven years old—this scene is still vivid to me. Finally he was invited to come back to us whenever he was in need again. In the meanwhile on inquiry Father found out that this poor man, all alone in the world, used to lodge in a barn, and beg his bread at the entrance of the military barracks. After several attempts and formalities my father succeeded in having him accepted by the Little Sisters of the Poor.

Many persons in need were thus helped, in particular an aristocratic family reduced to poverty. My father had noticed the husband leaning sorrowfully against the grating of the Prefecture buildings, and seemingly in the greatest distress. After having relieved his immediate needs, Father found an honourable position for the head of the family. It was the son of that gentlemen who at the birth of Thérèse brought to our home a welcome for the baby, written in verse; it was from the pen of the grateful father.

Another debtor to his charity wrote:

> More kindly man who ever knew, of great and noble heart ?
> All who implore, to them he doth protection strong impart.
> Rendering kindly free largesse that cannot altered be,
> Taking for his device and motto always loyalty,
> Invariable his graciousness to one and all he shows ;
> No one in vain implores his help when storm of trial blows.

His friends, witnesses of such rare virtues, were unforgetably struck by his charity. Years afterwards, when reading *The Story of a Soul* in 1899 one of them wrote:[1]

---

[1] M. Christophe Desroziers.

" It is not without strong emotion that I
have found here the physical and moral
portrait of dear Louis, one of the men whom
I loved most in this world. I never met a
nobler heart, nor a more generous soul. It
is certainly from him that Sister Thérèse of
the Child Jesus inherited her nobility of
feeling."

Under the heading of his acts of charity—an
inexhaustible subject—I can only relate a few
of his kind deeds. Another example would be
the thorny matter of little Armandine, a child
exploited by two unworthy creatures, who
had by fraud put on the Religious Habit.
My mother having discovered the fraud
resolved to get the little girl free from the
servitude of her hard-hearted captors. But
these unworthy women appealed to the judicial
court which summoned my mother. My
father considered it his duty to go with her and
to help her. In her letters she relates this
whole story in detail and, one can feel, with
great emotion.

Both parents were very generous not alone
in giving sympathetic help to all poor people
at considerable inconvenience to themselves,
but also assisted them financially when they
needed it. My father always carried some
loose money in his pocket to distribute alms
to the beggars he might meet along the streets.

During his journey through Central Europe he wrote from Constantinople to my eldest sister: " Give, Marie, give something always."

Our parents took affectionate care also of the servants employed at home, treating them with consideration. The same care was extended to the lace-makers who worked on the Point d'Alençon for my mother. She visited their homes, and saw to it that they needed nothing. The Monastery of the Poor Clares was another object of their constant kindness, and benefited often from the results of my father's fishing expeditions. Later on his generous gifts went to the Carmel of Lisieux.

If on his way through the streets he met an intoxicated man, he gave the man his arm and helped him home, accompanying his charitable act with a good remonstrance. Once he came across a drunken workman, who had fallen into the stream. When he helped the man up, he himself carried the tool-box, and led the man home. Another time having seen in the railway station a poor epileptic who had not enough money for his fare, Father took off his hat, placed an offering in it, and went round to all the passengers begging for him. Then after collecting the price for the journey, he settled the man in the railway carriage himself.

I was edified another time by an act of charity

of a different and more hidden kind. We had been out for a walk in the country when, as we neared the town, my father went into a home which we did not recognize but which seemed well-known to him. I saw him giving a sum of money to the mother of the family, who was alone with her little children. Very much surprised, I asked him: "Papa, do you know her?" "Yes!" he replied, "she is an unfortunate woman, whom her husband abandons from time to time, and whom I help when that happens." Was it one of those needy households visited by the Conference of St. Vincent de Paul, of which my father was one of the most zealous members? I do not know, but this act made me think there were many other cases like hers.

Besides he could not see any kind of misery without trying to relieve it. One morning he met at the church an old man who appeared worn out. Father asked him to come to Les Buissonnets, and gave him a good meal. As the old man was expressing his gratitude and begging God's blessings, my father made Thérèse and me kneel down at his feet in order to receive the poor man's blessing. We were then both grown-up girls; our elder sisters had already entered the convent.

His charity shone out also in a different way, as the following beautiful testimony after his death shows:

> "His charity was most admirable; he never expressed an unkind judgment in regard to anyone, and always found an excuse for the wrong-doing of a neighbour."

This spontaneous eulogy from his Alençon friends, who had always known him, was printed on his mortuary card. The Archpriest of the Cathedral admitted that it was a correct summing up of his life.

In this connection a little incident comes to my mind. My father's teeth were perfect and I saw him go to a dentist only once for an extraction. In spite of all the dentist's efforts he could not even move the tooth. Father, realizing that the dentist was disturbed about his professional reputation, if this should become known, then kindly said: "I shall not mention it to a soul!" And he kept his word.

His patience too was unalterable. Once he went with me to collect the house-rent from a tenant; it was in the main street of Lisieux. The woman refused to pay, and ran after him crying insulting things. I was horrified, but he remained calm and made no reply at all, and he did not complain about her afterwards. Frequently I had occasion to admire the great self-control he possessed, or rather which he had acquired, for by temperament he was quick.

They used to tell at home that at the time of

the German occupation in 1870 Father protested against the conduct of a Prussian soldier who was stealing a watch from the shop. Father sent an official complaint. But having heard that another soldier had been court-marshalled and shot for having stolen eggs, he withdrew his complaint immediately.

During our pilgrimage to Rome his kindly charity often attained heroic degrees. He excused and patiently bore with others, and tried to be always agreeable to them. He did not complain, no matter what the circumstances were, and as Thérèse relates, he showed the bright side of things, particularly to a grumbling old gentleman who had a mania for finding fault with everything.

I admired him very much when he made excuses for us on the train in regard to card games in which someone else wanted us to take part. We were young and eager to enjoy all the scenery, as Papa pointed it out. Besides he slipped in a word about the recitation of pilgrimage prayers, which exciting card parties sometimes prevented. One of the players was offended, and said with ill-humour: " Fortunately, Pharisees are rare! " Father closed his eyes without saying a word, as if he had not heard. Afterwards he showed himself very kind towards that gentleman, as ny saintly little sister points out. " After the

example of St. Francis de Sales he had completely
mastered his natural impetuosity of character
to such an extent that he appeared to be the
meekest person in the world."

MORTIFICATION AND HUMILITY

Father's spirit of penance extended to
everything. When we arrived at Lisieux there
was the question of bread to be considered, as
the bread was different from what we were
accustomed to at Alençon. We found what
was called the " soft " bread, and a kind of rye
bread as " hard " as a stone. In the beginning,
my sisters gave him the " soft " bread; but soon
he wanted the " hard " bread, because it was a
penance, and also because it was the bread
of the poor.

Looking back after all these years, I can see
how great our youthful inexperience was. In
learning about new vegetables, or sauces of
which I did not know the recipe, I have often
said to myself: " If I had given that to Papa,
how happy I could have made him! " Then I
recall what I had noticed in those days: that he
never made any comments about what we gave
him, whether it was well or badly prepared, and
he would on no account suggest what things
he liked best. He was in fact so forgetful
of himself in that respect that if he had been
alone I believe he would have had neither fire

nor cooking, and would have contented himself with a bit of bread, cheese and sausage.

At Les Buissonnets, although he had no taste for gardening, he considered it a duty to dig up and plant the garden at the back of the house. In warm weather, when we used to take him out some refreshing drink, for which he never would have asked if it were in Lent, there had to be " ifs " and " buts " to make him accept it. We used all our eloquence in assuring him that liquids do not break the fast, and that it was God who sent it to him. On Good Friday every year he took no supper.

Because of our lack of practical judgment we had not thought of putting blinds or curtains at the windows of his dear Belvedere, no doubt because they were of coloured glass. Facing the south and under the roof it became like a hothouse in summer. When it was too hot he went elsewhere for shelter rather than complain.

Seeing that he did not smoke cigarettes like our uncle, M. Guérin, we asked him once: " Papa, why do you not take a cigarette as all the other men do? " With a pleasant smile he replied: " Must we not practice a little mortification? " Doubtless also for the same reason, he did not cross his legs, and avoided making himself too comfortable or too relaxed; yet there was nothing stiff or stilted in his manner. Everything about him was simple, without pose or affectation.

As Thérèse wrote of him: " He was gifted with a natural distinction." This judgment was confirmed by Marie in her personal notes: " Papa was very fine looking, and had a rare natural distinction." " The air of a Cavalier ! " said someone who had known him. Essentially humble, he did not desire to attract attention, nor mix in worldly affairs. We rather pitied the Guérin family which was obliged for social reasons, on New Year's Day, etc., to receive and to make many visits.

Regarding his choice of the very first Mass at six o'clock whenever he was alone, when we asked him about it, he simply replied: " Because it is the Mass of the poor and the working people." Whenever he went on a journey, he travelled third class for the same reason, and because it was less comfortable. For him everything was always all right, and I do not remember even once having heard him complain if anything disagreeable turned up. It must be said that we also admired the same self-denial in our mother, who was just as forgetful of self. How often I have seen her carefully preparing the family breakfast with the greatest care, while contenting herself with a bowl of broth, taken standing up and alone by herself, while serving the others.

And I too share in the feeling of our eldest sister, Marie, who with self-reproach exclaims in her personal notes: " And I, who was brought up in such an environment, and had before my eyes the practice of virtues even to an heroic degree! " With my father the tendency to mortification and to humility only increased with his years. Marie had to try to moderate his penances. Once secretly she took away from him the *Life of the Fathers of the Desert*, which she had imprudently loaned to him, and which stimulated him in this regard.

WORK AND DISINTERESTEDNESS

The life of our parents was simple, economical, without avarice, and hard-working, in order to supply the demands of their many children, to whom they sought to give above all a solid Christian education. What sacrifices they imposed upon themselves for this end!

My mother had a very active temperament. She was always busy. Her household duties, in addition to the overseeing of her lace-making enterprise, absorbed her, sometimes even to excess. Father helped her in every way he could, and she was astonished at his success in business matters. When he saw her over-tiring herself beyond measure, he insisted that she should take on more workers, and

even went so far as to suggest that she might
be obliged to give up the whole undertaking.
But when anyone tried to moderate her zeal,
either concerning the work or her cares as
a mother, she would not easily listen to
reason. Papa was often obliged to let her
go ahead. However, to be able to give up
more of his time to her lace-making enterprise
and to lighten her work of correspondence,
etc., he sold out his own jewelry shop.

Having great artistic taste himself, he could
thus more effectively help her, and he
transferred to his own name the manufacture
of the famous Point d'Alençon lace. With the
practical judgment which characterized him, he
was thorough in everything he undertook, or
considered his duty. So also he was very
severe in regard to any sign of negligence or
carelessness. As a result he made an excellent
business man, yet with great detachment and
without seeking to amass a fortune. I can see
in my mind yet the place on the street, where
he said to me one day: " I feel that I could easily
acquire a taste for investing, but I do not want
to be carried away by that current. It is such
a dangerous incline, and leads to speculating."

Consequently he devoted to his investments
only the care which was strictly necessary.
" Cast thy care upon the Lord," [1] as the sacred

---

[1] *Psalm* liv. 23.

writers recommend.   And the Lord was faithful to him.   Here is an example. His lawyer had proposed to him a financial transaction, which seemed very advantageous, and was going with him to Bordeaux, where the deal was to take place.   But on the very morning of the departure my father for no reason at all had some kind of a sprain. He saw in this an indication of Providence, and in spite of the insistence of the lawyer, who was then rapping at the front door, my father refused to set out on the journey.   A short time afterwards the whole enterprise collapsed.

That is why, having learned from experience, his confidence in God enabled him to visualize with serenity the possible loss of all his money. Thérèse relates in one of her letters how he used to say jokingly: " This is what we'll do when we become bankrupt! "   He often used to quote to us with conviction the passage of the *Imitation*: " Man's happiness consisteth not in having abundance of temporal goods, but a moderate portion is sufficient for him." [1] His disinterestedness was pointed out by my mother in regard to a sum of money in an estate, which a contractor claimed without sufficient proof.   She wrote to her brother Isidore who was also entangled in the affair: [2]

[1] *Imitation*, Book I, Chapter 22.
[2] January 3, 1872.

> " To be sure we paid it as well as the
> interest on this sum which had not been
> paid for eight years. My husband said to
> me: ' I do not want Isidore to pay his share,
> for he has always been so nice to you.'
> I just mention it to show how good Louis is."

My parents were always extremely happy in
this mutual family assistance. My mother
writes to her sister-in-law: [1]

> " My husband has decided to sell out a
> part of his Credit Foncier stocks at a loss
> of 1,300 francs. If my brother needs any
> money at present, let him ask for it
> immediately."

Owing to their hard work we were financially
in easy circumstances, but they did not seek
gain for its own sake. At Mamma's death
Father gave up all lucrative occupation, and
devoted himself entirely to his children. Besides
he could not continue the manufacture of the
Point d'Alençon which required a woman to
oversee it. However, at Lisieux he did not
lead an idle life; quite the contrary. He
divided his time between intellectual work,
household occupations, the administration of
his property, devotional exercises and our
education.

With his cultivated mind he loved reading.

[1] July 30, 1871.

As a young man *The Spirit of Christianity* by Chateaubriand had delighted him, and he tried to get a copy of this work. He made up a collection of "special selections," chosen and copied by him, of which he had learned a certain number by heart. In his collection of books were the following: *Studies in Christianity* by August Nicolas, *History of the People of God*, *Works of St. Alphonsus di Liguori*, all the volumes of the *Liturgical Year* by Dom Guéranger, etc. Every week our eldest sister, Marie, borrowed different books from the parish library. In that way he read many Lives of the Saints, and also historical works in which he took a great interest: *History of France*, *History of the Empire*, *History of the Church*, *The Reformer of La Trappe*, M. de Rancé, etc.

My father had no interest in novels. To entertain him Marie once brought him some, but he smilingly returned them to her. On the other hand he found poetry full of charm. He used to recite for us from memory long passages principally from Lamartine and Victor Hugo.

For his manual labour besides gardening at Les Buissonnets my father took over the care of the poultry yard and the rabbits, providing their food and not allowing anyone to help him in the cleaning of the yard. We had an aviary for pet birds, which he took care of as well. As an amusement for us, he succeeded in

teaching a tame magpie to speak. He also
took charge of the cellar, and bought apples
for cider, which he brewed at home himself.
Along with all that he sawed and chopped and
stacked in the laundry house all the firewood
that was required for the household. I
sometimes found him there, quite tired out in
later years. Up in the Belvedere I can still
see him working diligently with watch and
clock wheels. I made a sketch of him at that
work. I used to raise silk-worms, and to help
me in the winding-off of the cocoons he made
an ingenious little spinning-wheel. He invented
other playthings made with the rinds of melons,
oranges, or the pith of the elder tree. The little
melon-rind carts ran perfectly, and were most
attractive.

THE HEAD OF THE FAMILY AND THE EDUCATOR

Not only my father when he was young, but
my mother also, had desired to enter the
Religious Life. With the disappointment of
their hopes, they both turned towards the
married state, but aimed at realizing in it the
maximum of Christian Spirit.[1]

---

[1] A curious coincidence! It was on the anniversary of their
marriage, July 13, 1927, two years after the Canonization of their
last child, that Pius XI at the request of almost 400 Cardinals,
Archbishops and Superior Generals, extended by special privilege
to the Universal Church the Mass and Office of St. Thérèse
of the Child Jesus.

After having lived for many months as brother and sister, they then wished to have many children in order to offer them to God, a decision in which their Confessor and Spiritual Director encouraged them. One can understand how the priest who baptized their first baby was edified to hear my father saying with joy: "This is the first time that I have come here for a Baptismal Ceremony, but it will not be the last!" He returned there indeed nine times. At each one of these times he engraved on the inside of his watch-case the names and dates of his well-beloved children.

Between our parents there was a perfect agreement of heart and mind. My father often spoke to us of our "saintly mother," as he called her. On her part she wrote to her brother: "What a holy man my husband is! I wish every woman in the world could have his equal." [1] In her correspondence, likewise to Isidore, we read in reference to their aged father, M. Guérin: [2]

> "You know our father is a very fine man, but now he has developed the little vagaries of an elderly person; his children must bear with them, and my mind is quite made up about that.
>
> "Suggest to him not to engage any other

---

[1] January 1, 1863.
[2] November 18, 1866.

housekeeper and to come and live with us. My husband is quite willing for that arrangement. You could not find one in a hundred who would be so kind to a father-in-law."

Naturally a constant admirer of his fine qualities, my mother was unhappy when her husband was away, and she concluded a letter addressed to him in Paris where he had gone on business:

> " I am so happy to-day at the thought of welcoming you back again, that I cannot work for the joy of it.—Your wife who loves you more than her life! " [1]

On another occasion, she writes to him from Lisieux. She was at her brother's with the two elder girls. All were just about to leave for the seashore, and having all kinds of parties.

> " The children are enchanted, but I find it hard to relax. None of this has any interest for me. I feel exactly like the fish that you pull out of the water; they are no longer in their element, they must perish.
> " I should be like them if I had to stay much longer. I feel so much out of sorts— which affects me physically. All day long

[1] 1869.

I am with you in spirit. I say to myself:
' he is doing such and such a thing now.'

" I long so much to be back with you again,
my dear Louis. I love you with all my
heart, and I feel my affection redoubled by
the privation of the need I feel of your
presence. It would be impossible for me
to live separated from you." [1]

In July 1871 at the time of moving to the
new dwelling-house on the Rue St. Blaise,
where Thérèse was to be born, she expresses
her complete satisfaction:

" We are perfectly settled in our new home.
My husband has arranged the house just the
way I should like to have it."

And later on after a medical examination,
in which the doctor did not conceal the gravity
of the malady which was to prove fatal, she
writes: [2]

" My husband is inconsolable. He has
entirely given up the pleasure of fishing, and
has put away his fishing-rods in the barn.
He does not wish either to go to the Vital
Club;[3] he is quite crushed."

---

[1] August 31, 1873.
[2] December 17, 1876.
[3] The Vital Romet Circle.

Their union, so perfect and complete, was spiritualized and directed altogether to the thought of eternal life. That can be gathered from a remark made at the time of the illness of our sister Léonie. During her two first years she was almost always between life and death. At the recommendation of our Visitation aunt, Sister Marie-Dosithée, the intercession of Blessed Margaret Mary was invoked. "If little Léonie is to become a saint some day, we beg her cure," was the condition given by the parents. Almost immediately an improvement rewarded their faith. It is not surprising then that on the occasion of the publication of *The Story of a Family* our Holy Father Pius XII in a letter to Mother Agnes of Jesus, praised this book, "which describes, and in a certain way resurrects that admirable family life . . . and holds up for the homes of to-day such an appropriate example to stimulate them in the entire practice of the Christian Virtues." [1]

* * *

On re-reading my deposition at the Apostolic Process for the Beatificaion of our saintly little Thérèse I find the following testimony in regard to my father:

---

[1] October 5, 1949.

> " Hard as he was on himself, he was
> always affectionate towards us. His heart
> was exceptionally tender towards us. He
> lived for us alone. No mother's heart
> could surpass his. Still with all that
> there was no weakness. All was just and
> well-regulated."

In her *Autobiography* Thérèse also points out
that after the death of our mother " Papa's
affectionate heart seemed truly endowed with
a mother's love." This motherly care was
noticed by persons outside. Canon Lepelletier,[1]
who was, as I already said, my father's confessor,
wrote to us in 1910:

> " I love to recall the happy moments that
> I spent at Les Buissonnets with your father
> who was so holy, and his very dear children."

The following is one of many examples
of the watchfulness which he displayed for
us from the cradle. As I was born after the
death of my two little brothers, I was confided
to a nurse at Alençon itself, in order to keep
me as near as possible to our home. My foster-
mother was remarkable for her orderliness and
cleanliness. In spite of that Papa was very

---

[1] Assistant priest at the Cathedral in Lisieux, then P.P. and
Dean of St. Stephen's, Caen.

anxious, and purposely used to walk up and down in front of her house. I was only a few weeks old when one day he heard me crying convulsively. He entered and found me in the cradle all alone. He searched around the house and inquired from the neighbours; the nurse had gone—for a drink! He learned then that she was often drunk, and did not nourish me sufficiently. Already puny I was dying of neglect. I was therefore taken away from there and was sent to the country, this time to be nursed by a good, decent woman. It was only after a thousand mishaps that I gradually grew strong. My mother wrote:[1] " I have had so much anxiety on account of this child that I feel worn out."

It is sufficient to read my mother's letters to realize how much my father had at heart the desire to help her in all her anxieties, whether it was to set out at four o'clock in the morning to find a wet-nurse for a sick baby, or on another occasion to accompany her a distance of six miles from Alençon on a freezing cold night to the cradle of their dying little Joseph.[2] Again he watched for days and weeks as a sick-nurse beside their eldest child, Marie, who at the age of thirteen was suffering from typhoid-fever.[3]

---

[1] August 20, 1869.
[2] Letters of October 1879 and of January 1867.
[3] Letter of April 10, 1873.

That devoted tenderness of his became still more evident when we moved to Lisieux. After the death of our mother a very important question arose for him with regard to his five daughters, the eldest of whom was seventeen and the youngest only four and a half. Many friends, even his Spiritual Director, advised him to place us all as boarding pupils. Again he had influential relatives and friends among the upper classes of Alençon, and all urged him not to leave the town. Besides, was he not too advanced in years to change all his ways, to uproot himself, so to speak, and begin a wholly new life? With his outspoken ways my uncle, M. Guérin, rather frightened my father, who was by nature so simple and reserved. It would be introducing the " Patriarch " into quite a wholly different environment.

But the love of his children had first place in his heart. He sought their welfare, their greatest welfare, without taking his own into consideration. It was on that account, after having consulted his older girls, that he made the decision to go to Lisieux in order to be nearer the influence of Madame Guérin, an angel of peace and of sweetness. " I ask your advice, children," he said, " for it is solely on your account I am making this sacrifice, and I do not wish to impose a sacrifice on you."

In after years I wanted to know why he decided

to leave Alençon in spite of the contrary views that were presented to him. He wished, he replied, " to take us away from influences that he considered too worldly among some of his friends, and from the liberal ideas of others." How grateful we should be to him for a decision so wise and so disinterested!

In agreement with our mother he decided that all his children, even the two little Josephs, should have " Marie " as their first Baptismal name. He had suggested that, as in his own family, the children should address their parents with the more formal " vous," instead of the more intimate " tu," but Mamma objected that formal attitudes and phrases might give the impression of distance, and that she " would feel herself less loved," and he agreed immediately.

In the intimacy of home life he often called us by affectionate or characteristic nicknames. Marie was " the diamond," sometimes " the gypsy " on account of her independent spirit. Pauline was " the fine pearl," then came " good-hearted Léonie." I was " the dauntless one." As for Thérèse, she was in turn " the Little Queen of France and Navarre," " the Orphan of the Berezina," the " little blonde May-beetle," or the " Bouquet."

Certainly he was altogether charmed by his Benjamin; our mother herself says so complacently. " He adores that child," she wrote, " he does everything she wants." It was to please him, too, that the beautiful flaxen hair of our little sister used to be curled. But a precious testimony given in the Canonical Process by a former housemaid in my uncle's home, who afterwards became a Benedictine Nun, refutes the objection of those who imagined that our father spoiled her. This maid stated:

> " M. Martin was an excellent father, and he educated his children, all of whom he loved very much, with the greatest care. The Servant of God, Thérèse, whom he called his ' little Queen,' being the youngest, was the object of his special affection, but this did not lessen in any way the serious tone of his education of her. He would not tolerate any fault in her. Without being severe, he raised his children in fidelity to all their duties."

I believe I struck the right note on this point in my own deposition at the Apostolic Process:

> " My father had a very special consideration for his youngest child, and was as attentive to her as a mother. But if it is true that little Thérèse was, as she says, always ' surrounded with love,' it is also true that she was never spoiled. The proof that my father did not spoil her, and that she did

not do just what she liked at home, is
shown by a fact which made a deep
impression on her, and which she relates in
her *Autobiography*: how she was severely
reprimanded for not wishing to leave her
games at the first call of her father.

"A little later, at Lisieux—she might have
been six years old—she took great pleasure
in carrying the newspaper to our father every
morning.   One day I wanted to take it to
him; but Thérèse, quicker than I, had already
caught it up and ran to him.   This disappointed
me and I showed it.   Papa reproached little
Thérèse for not having yielded to me, and
he scolded her very severely, so much so
that I was extremely upset myself."

In *The Story of a Soul* other examples are found
which at the same time show his tenderness
and his firmness towards Thérèse.   She has
related in her manuscript how after the death
of our mother he surrounded her with the
most tender care.   Every day at the end of
the classes given her by Pauline she used to go
up to the Belvedere to show to her "dear
King" the rosette and the notes given her by
her teacher.   It was her joy to cry to him:
"Papa, I have full marks for everything.   Pauline
said so first!"

In the afternoon she used to go for a walk
with him and a visit to the Blessed Sacrament.

It was on one of these occasions that he showed her the Carmelite chapel and the sanctuary-grille, behind which the nuns were praying. In the garden of Les Buissonnets she used to dance around him; make him close his eyes while she was arranging her " marvellous altars," then she would cry enthusiastically, " Papa, open your eyes—look! "

" Ah! " she wrote at the end of her life, " how could I relate all the tenderness lavished by Papa on his ' little Queen ' ? There are things which the heart feels and which no human words or thoughts could express." However, when she fell sick at Les Buissonnets, and it seemed to be a fatal illness, the faith and resignation of my father were admirable. Finally it was he who had a Novena of Masses offered for her at the Sanctuary of Our Lady of Victories in Paris, putting into that his last hope. The result is given in *Our Lady of the Smile!* In the " Prayer of the Child of a Saint," Thérèse recalls that paternal predilection, breathing heavenly fragrance:

Remember thou that on the terrace green
   Her place was often on thy saintly knees;
And murmuring a prayer for her, " thy Queen,"
   Thou didst sing softly in the Sunday breeze.
And she, upon thy heart, saw in thy holy face
   A shining of Heaven's light, a strange unearthly
      grace.

The beauty, sung by thee,
  Was of eternity!
    Remember thou!

*   *   *

At home our education had piety as its chief lever. There was a complete liturgy of household life: evening prayers all together, Month of May Devotions, Sunday Offices, spiritual reading before the Feasts, etc. Our father aided as much as he could the development of the spiritual life. Thus several times he accompanied Marie to see her Spiritual Director, Father Pichon. Once in 1886 he gave her himself a little lesson of Spirituality. They had gone to Calais, then crossed to Dover, in order to await the boat, which was to bring the Jesuit priest back from Canada. But neither priest nor boat arrived. Marie was frightfully annoyed at her disappointment, but Father said quietly: " We should not complain, Marie. Our Lord has seen good to send you this trial, and I am happy to be His instrument in making this journey with you."

Our venerable father was careful to avert from us anything that might disturb our souls. Every morning when we were going to early Mass, he used to tell us not to be looking up at the windows, which in summer would be open, lest we see persons dressing, or half-dressed.   On our walks in the country if perchance we passed a bathing-place, he would tell us to look in another direction.   He would never tolerate, either for himself or for anyone in the house, a careless appearance, or any lack of modesty in dress.   We should not have dared, in his presence, to have had short-sleeved dresses, only just to the elbow.   What would he say of the world to-day?   All vulgar or slang words were rigidly forbidden.   At meals he held strictly to the rules of etiquette.   There was no making of faces or showing repugnance if one did not like a dish.   " No soup, no meat," he used to say smilingly, to encourage us " to eat our soup."   During Lent there were some restrictions in the fare at table.

Very exact himself, Papa taught us: " Never put off till to-morrow what you can do to-day," and all was to be done punctually.   Again he would never allow bills to remain unpaid for any time; it was " never credit, always cash." He wished us to be always busy.   In order to develop our tastes and talents he spared nothing to procure all sorts of material that might be needed or pleasant for our art work, either embroidery or painting: for instance, special thread for lace-making, little shells of gold for painting, sheets of ivory or parchment for Pauline's miniatures.

Self-love was completely put aside, even in its slightest manifestations. The mortuary notice on Sister Marie du Sacré-Cœur, published after her death, contains the following incident of her childhood:

> "One year at the end of the summer holidays Marie was taking a walk with our father in a small family property, which formerly belonged to a person called Roullée. Marie began to gather some flowers saying: 'I will take these back with me to the Visitation School, as a souvenir of the Roullées.' Our father, wishing to teach her a lesson, replied: 'That's it! And then you can look down on your little friends by showing them the flowers from your estate.' Poor Marie, seeing that he had guessed her thoughts, threw away her bouquet to show that she was above vainglory."

Our father was a keen observer, a good psychologist, and had a wonderful insight into persons and things. Always faithful to his religious convictions, he wished to confide our instruction to truly Christian teachers. He sent the two older girls to the Visitation Nuns at Le Mans, and later confided Léonie, Thérèse and myself to the Benedictine Nuns at Lisieux. At that time school-children were never allowed to go alone, and young girls of our environment were always accompanied. Truly it was servitude. Every morning someone had to go with us and call for us in the evening, for we were half-boarding pupils. Sometimes it was the maid, but often Papa was asked to take his turn. He did it willingly, but nevertheless one could see that it was through virtue. If we had only average reports for our class-work, he showed that he was not quite pleased, and we were mortified on seeing his displeasure.

He liked order, and carried it out himself very strictly. When something was broken through negligence he showed his disapproval rather severely. On the other hand he allowed us the widest latitude in the management of the house, although this was left at first to Marie, the oldest girl, who was only seventeen, and later on to me when I was about the same age. I noticed that he always avoided interfering with our arrangements. If we had forgotten something, or made some mistake, he seemed to take no notice of it, in order not to make us nervous or timid, according to the recommendation of St. Paul. Finally, he was a big man, not alone physically, but in every way—a fine noble character, if there ever was one! And all that made us perfectly happy.

INCOMPARABLE FATHER

That is the expression of Thérèse herself in her manuscript, but each of us at one time or another used it in our letters, for we admired our father so much that we had truly a veneration, almost a worship for him; he was so good, so holy.   By character very cheerful, he knew how to brighten our home-life. He possessed a store of proverbs full of good sense, of amusing stories, of old songs which he sang or recited as occasion arose.   All this made him the most delightful company. In the intimacy of Les Buissonnets there was at all times a note of true and healthy joy. We were completely self-sufficing in our entertainments, and did not usually leave our own family group except to go to some evening party at the Catholic Circle.   But that was rare.

No one could surpass him as the life of our home-parties.   He knew how to come down to our level, and to take an interest in our games as, it is told, Henry IV or Napoleon did in other days.   Sometimes he deftly rolled along the floor pretty gilt marbles, or again he beat out military marches with his finger-tips in perfect time.   At other times he would hide surprises in the garden and follow our searches by the words: " You're hot," or else " you're cold," as we either neared the objects or not.   Again he would hold something very high beyond our reach, exclaiming: " For the first person to say Amen." I have already noted that he even constructed playthings for us, for he was very ingenious in that respect. In the evening in our childhood days at Alençon the reflector of a street-lamp cast a shadow across the street. In order to amuse us he used to take us in his arms one after the other to pass through the shade and light.

He was gifted with a very beautiful voice, and it was a real pleasure to listen to him as he sang or recited. Often too he imitated the whistling or varied singing of the birds. He was also a perfect mimic, and Thérèse must have learned that art from him which, it is only right to add, she like our father always used with charity and tact. In the writings of the Saint, as in the letters of all the family, we come across snatches of those songs or proverbs borrowed from our father. Many of them are in the dialect of Normandy, or Auvergne. He had them for every occasion. " In the struggles and collisions of life, we must imitate the travellers, Tombi, Carabi: get up again after each fall and always keep looking up." An excellent billiard-player, he used to repeat masterfully, " Here below we must play our best ball well," or, imitating the Marseilles

accent, " This life is a ' theeáyter,' everybody
acts his own part, my dear! "

Is it surprising that Thérèse, speaking in my
name in her poem, " What I used to Love,"
expressed the charms of such a wonderful
father?

Theresa, seated on his knee,
Listened with me there, tenderly,
To those melodious songs he sang for me.
Those accents sweet I can not yet
Forget.
O Memory, what joys you bring!
You make the thought of many a thing
That flew from me, long since, like birds awing.
Faces I see, voices I hear,
How dear!

With what enthusiasm we annually celebrated
Papa's Feastday of St. Louis! We went up to
the Belvedere which was decked out for the
occasion with flowers and garlands. Thérèse
would recite a compliment in verse composed
by Pauline. We then offered him some simple
present. Naturally our Carmelite sisters joined
in also and sent an affectionate spiritual message.
Sister Marie du Sacré-Cœur wrote on August 24,
1886:

" Sister Agnes of Jesus who is the artistic
miniature painter, and occasionally the house-
painter, has inscribed on the walls of

Reverend Mother's cell[1] this beautiful passage from the Psalms:[2] *The Lord conducted the just . . . in a wonderful way: and was to them for a covert by day and for the light of stars by night.* Everything beautiful that I see I find applies to you."

For August 25, 1885, it was to Vienna that the " Little Queen " addressed her poetical good wishes to her " King-Papa." That year he had undertaken a long tour of Europe, as far as the Bosphorus; he had planned also to go to Jerusalem, and to return by Italy. As a companion he had Father Marie, a priest of St. James's parish, who like our father loved to travel. Our dear father always had been attracted by the call of the Holy Land as well as of Rome, and to go there he almost asked our permission. In the course of their trip they had to renounce the visit to the Holy Land; and they were unable to have a Papal Audience. Although we felt keenly the absence of him who was indeed our life and our joy, we nevertheless could only encourage him to enjoy that relaxation, since he was always so forgetful of self for us.[3]

---

[1] Allusion to Scriptural texts written on the walls of the monastery.

[2] *Wisdom* x. 10, 17.

[3] See in the Appendix his letters at that time.

He used to repeat with a note of satisfaction and pride: " I am the *bobillon* with my children," that is, tender and kindly. In our advancing years my sisters and I used to love to say very softly to each other, referring to our father's expression, that our Heavenly Father, the Lord God Himself, has always been " bobillon " towards us.

To complete this moral portrait, even at the risk of repetition, let me quote a passage from my Deposition for the Beatification Process of Thérèse:

> " My father was a very simple and upright character. Physically and morally he had the appearance of a Patriarch. There was also another striking resemblance: I remember that when he used to take me to the Benedictine School, my teachers, the nuns, used to say he reminded them of St. Joseph. Indeed he was truly a *just man*, and when I wish to picture what St. Joseph was like, I just like to think of my father."

Our little Thérèse has declared likewise:

> " If an earthly father can be so ideal, what must our Heavenly Father be like. . .! "

In granting her an incomparable father whose

goodness was a first picture of the goodness of
Our Father in Heaven, Our Lord was preparing
her to penetrate, more than anyone else, into
the mystery of the divine Paternity. This gave
her that filial piety towards God upon which
her " Little Way of Spiritual Childhood "
entirely revolves. Yes, I humbly confess, our
devout parents well merited to give to the
world this " Little Thérèse "; pious pilgrims
have inscribed on their tomb this acknowledge-
ment of gratitude, an *ex voto* in letters of gold:

> " Thank you, dear Christian parents, for
> having given us a little saint to protect us."

This is the *Little Thérèse* whose Cause of
Beatification Blessed Pius X opened; whose
doctrine of Spiritual Childhood Benedict XV
exalted. This is the *Little Thérèse* whom
Pius XI canonized and declared Patroness of
the Missions; and whom he called a " living
word of God " and " the cherished child of the
whole world "; finally, whom Pius XII declared
Patroness of France, with St. Joan of Arc. It
is quite right to apply to them the words of the
Gospel:[1] " Wherefore by their fruits you shall
know them."

---

[1] *Matthew* vii. 20.

OUR FATHER OFFERS ALL HIS CHILDREN
TO GOD

Our devout parents had each of them wished to enter the Religious Life, and God had decided otherwise, but they wished at least to offer a priest to the Lord, a missionary priest. Alas! what disappointment they must have felt when after the death of my two little brothers I was born, the fifth of their little girls. In the secret of their hearts they persisted nevertheless in hoping for that blessing of God for their home, which had been saddened by the loss of the two little boys. The Visitation Nun of Le Mans encouraged them:

> " The Lord wished to claim the first-fruits (the sons) to try their faith, but assuredly He would crown their hopes in granting them the *great saint* they longed for so much."

However, after me another little daughter came into the family circle, only to fly off almost immediately to Heaven. Then came the seventh girl, the ninth and last child, Thérèse! Humanly speaking they had done all that depended on them to give God a missionary priest. Their hopes seemed to be frustrated, and yet there was no expression of regret. Above all they lived in entire abandonment to God, and surrendered themselves completely to divine Providence. The word of the Psalmist was the spontaneous utterance of their own hearts: " I will bless the Lord at all times; His praise will be forever on my lips " (*Ps.* xxxiii. 2).

Disappointed with regard to the priesthood, our mother then desired to see all her daughters consecrated in the Religious Life. She died prematurely, and it was our good father who carried out the offering, as he generously accepted the vocation of all five of them. Certainly our environment, which was profoundly Christian, lent itself to this religious appeal. But our parents never influenced us in that direction. Mamma had rightly foreseen that Pauline would enter the convent. Thérèse refers to this in her *Autobiography*, and attributes to the first announcement of Pauline's vocation, as yet only dimly comprehended by her, her own first desire for the Religious Life. At Les Buissonnets however none of us ever thought of Carmel. The Carmelite Monastery of Lisieux inspired us rather with fear, with its grilles and the mortuary urns that ornamented the entrance door.

Our father had expected that his second daughter, Pauline, would join the Visitation Nuns at Le Mans, where our aunt had lived and had died a saintly death. But unexpectedly on February 16, 1882, after a signal grace which

she received in St. James's Church, Pauline
announced her desire to enter Carmel.   Our
father made no objection; he simply inquired
if her health would adapt itself to such an austere
Rule.   Speaking with her alone in the afternoon,
he said to her: "I have allowed you to go to
Carmel for your greater happiness; however,
do not imagine that it will not cost me a sacrifice,
for I love you very much."   He accompanied
her himself to the Monastery on the following
October 2nd, and led her to the Altar for her
Clothing Day on April 6, 1883.   At that time,
as later for Thérèse, the postulant clothed in
a white bridal gown came out of the cloister
to be received before the Choir grille.

On May 8, 1884, the evening of the Profession
of Sister Agnes of Jesus, which according to
the Constitutions took place in presence of the
nuns alone, he took little Thérèse, who had
made her First Communion that same day in
the chapel of the Benedictine Nuns, to see her
at the Carmel parlour.   The following July 16th
he assisted in the Sanctuary in front of the Choir
grille at the Veiling Ceremony of Sister Agnes.
In all these circumstances he showed great
faith and admirable fortitude.

* * *

As Marie was to join Sister Agnes of Jesus
in Carmel in October, 1886, Father wished

her to make a last pilgrimage to the tomb of our dear mother; and we four sisters went to Alençon with him.   There suddenly Léonie in a visit to the Poor Clares, confided to the Mother Abbess her desire of being admitted into the Community, and even of entering immediately.   When our dear father had to tell us about her decision, he appeared embarrassed.   Marie was very annoyed and showed it.   Thérèse and I were both much grieved.   As for our father, as patient as he was supernatural, he excused our sister as well as he could, for he was charity itself.

Afterwards we went to see Léonie behind the grille, dressed in the Habit of postulants. We did not believe that she could persevere. In fact she was obliged for reasons of health to leave a few weeks afterwards on December 12th. Our father did not say a word of rebuke to her; on the contrary he consoled and encouraged her with the greatest sympathy.

As to our eldest sister, it must be confessed that Papa had a soft spot for her in his heart, although it was never at the expense of the others.   He called her his " big girl," his " first." She managed the household, and had never shown the slightest attraction for the Religious Life.   Being very independent by nature, she had instead more of an aversion for it.   In spite of that she confided fully in Father Pichon, and our father accompanied her to Brittany that she might make a retreat preached by the saintly Jesuit there.

Marie herself has told how she began gradually to think of Carmel.   When she broached the subject to our dear father, he heaved a deep sigh in a sort of bewilderment.   " Ah! Ah! but without you. . ."   He overcame his emotion, embraced her, and then said: " I thought that you would never leave me! "   In the depths of his soul he was proud of her vocation.

In a letter which she wrote to me from Carmel, July 23, 1891, Marie, then Sister Marie du Sacré Cœur, reminded me of an amusing saying of our father when one of his daughters gave herself to God: " I understand better now," she wrote, " the thought of our dear father, who used to say with his direct simplicity: " *That's another one freed from the shafts of the cart.*" [1]   Oh! yes, another one who will take her flight to the heights.   Another who will " follow the Lamb whithersoever He goeth! " [2]

My father took Marie to Carmel for the Feast of St. Teresa, October 15, 1886.   The following year on the Feast of St. Joseph he assisted at her Clothing Ceremony, at which Father Pichon preached a very beautiful sermon on the Religious Life.   At the conclusion

[1] Allusion to cows pulling carts in Normandy.
[2] *Apoc.* xiv. 4.

of these ceremonies my father usually gave a dinner for the clergy, at which he himself was also present, at the rectory of the parish priest of St. James's, Canonical Superior of the Carmel. On the occasion of Marie's Clothing the Rev. Father Godefroy Madelaine, Prior of the Premonstratensians, was present. It was he who was to correct the manuscript of Thérèse and was to be called the "godfather of *The Story of a Soul*." He testified that my father sat near him at the table, and said to him:

> "I am very happy indeed. Those are two of my daughters whose salvation is assured. I have another who is not yet fourteen, and is already all on fire to join them."

It may be truly said that he lived in spirit with his Carmelites as much as he lived with us at home. He loaded them with presents, and his daughters thanked him in the name of the whole Community. That is what I find in a letter of Sister Marie du Sacré Cœur, of 1887:

> "This evening it was I who read in the refectory. As I was reading the Gospel for to-morrow, where our Lord appeared to the Apostles, and ate broiled fish with them, our Mother[1] stopped me in the reading to

---

[1] Rev. Mother Marie de Gonzague.

say to the community that it was you who were to supply the fish to-morrow for the Community.

"Thus, dearest father, you will do for us what Jesus did long ago for the Apostles. How good He was to them! And how good you are to us! He loved Peter the fisherman very much. One day He filled the net of Peter to such an extent that it almost broke with the catch.

"But St. Peter is not the only privileged person. I know another old fisherman whose net is almost breaking. And Jesus so loves His old fisherman that He asks him the whole fruit of his catch: all his children for Himself.

"Ah! He cannot bestow a greater honour. He cannot prove better how much He cherishes him.

"And so the old fisherman understands the words of his Master! How like St. Peter he is! From his boat he rushes to the shore. He echoes the word of St. John: 'It is the Lord!' How the Lord blesses him! And in Heaven will crown him with glory."

* * *

The vocation of Thérèse was the supreme offering for Papa. She had told me of her wish to enter Carmel at fifteen. But how could she speak of it to her "Dearest King"? He would have to sacrifice the last shred of his poor heart.   Besides he had an attack of illness on May 1st; although he quickly recovered, he nevertheless remained paler and less robust.

Léonie had asked him for permission to make a fresh trial at the Visitation of Caen, and he had consented immediately.   To be sure, he had an inkling of the secret desire of his " Queen."   That can be seen from his remark to Father Godefroy Madelaine, to which I have referred.   It can be gathered also from the description given by Thérèse in her manuscript, of the interview of Sunday, May 29, 1887. Before Thérèse spoke to him he held her pressed to his heart, guessing what she was going to say.   He encouraged her to speak, and when she had expressed her desire, he wholeheartedly said " Yes."

> " Papa," wrote Thérèse, " seemed to enjoy the quiet peace of a sacrifice performed.   He spoke to me as a saint; I would wish to recall his words and write them here, but I have only a memory that remains too fragrant to be analysed in human words."

Our little sister was to meet more difficulties on the part of our uncle Guérin, who gave his consent only in October.   It was preferable that our father let her handle the matter directly with our uncle without his intervention. On the other hand he accompanied her to see Father Delatroëtte, pastor of St. James's, and Superior of the Carmel. They were coldly received. This worthy priest had been severely criticized by people, because one of his spiritual children, belonging to an important family of Lisieux, wished to enter the Carmelite Monastery. He did not wish to expose himself to a renewal of the same attacks for a child of fifteen.

Our Father, believing that the Bishop would take part in the diocesan pilgrimage to Rome, which we also were to join, encouraged Thérèse, and promised that he would present her to His Excellency during the trip. But on the advice of Sister Agnes of Jesus he decided to go with her to Bayeux and to see Msgr. Hugonin personally with her. This visit took place on October 31, 1887. His "fine pearl" wrote to him touchingly at that time:

> "All Carmel is praying for the father of our lily, for that fruitful tree which produces nothing but virgin-souls. . .
>
> "If you only knew how my heart goes out to you, in thinking of all that you want to do for your 'little Queen'—of all that you have done for us! Ah! never fear, ingratitude

does not exist in Carmel: we shall not
forget the benefits we owe to you, and the
good God is counting them all.   What a
crown he is preparing for you! "

During the audience with the Bishop, Father
generously took the part of Thérèse, to the
great admiration of the Bishop and his Vicar
General, Abbé Révérony; but the results
remained negative.

*   *   *

On the following November 4, we left Les
Buissonnets to join in Paris all the pilgrims
for Rome; the departure was scheduled for
the 7th.   Always eager to give us pleasure
Papa wished first to show us around the capital.
He was full of life and cheerfulness.   I need
not relate in detail the long, splendid journey
which is described in *The Story of a Soul*.   Our
pilgrimage had been decided upon before the
disappointment of Bayeux.   Contrary to what
some persons believe, the object of the
pilgrimage for us was not to afford to Thérèse
an occasion of soliciting from the Pope the
authorization which had been refused her by
the Superiors.   She had thought of it indeed
before leaving, but Carmel had dissuaded her
at first, and she had submissively renounced the

idea. Always the obedient child, it was owing to new instructions from Carmel communicated to her by her " Little Mother " on our arrival in Rome, that she undertook her courageous endeavour with the approval of our father.

The Pontifical Audience took place on Sunday, November 20. First we all assisted at the Mass of Leo XIII in the Hall of the Consistory. Outside we could hear the beating rain, thunder and lightning. In her descriptions Thérèse gives a misleading impression in the order of the presentation of the pilgrims. For each diocese in turn, Coutances, Bayeux, Nantes, the ladies passed first before the Holy Father, so that Papa was not presented until after us. I quote here the greater part of the letter which I wrote the same day to Sister Marie:

" When our turn came to kneel at the feet of the Holy Father, Thérèse knelt down, but unfortunately it was Abbé Révérony who was with the pilgrims from Bayeux, and it was he who presented them to the Sovereign Pontiff. When Thérèse made her request with tears in her eyes the Holy Father bent down and said: ' I do not understand very well.' You know he is so old that it would make one weep just to look at him; he is as pale as death. He can scarcely hold himself up and speak; he seems broken with age, but what a beautiful expression! He is truly a *Holy Father*.

"But to come back to the request of Thérèse. Abbé Révérony replied immediately in a tone of irony, ' It is a child who asks to enter Carmel at fifteen; but the question is being examined by the Superiors.' Then the Holy Father replied, after the repetition of Thérèse's request: ' My dear child, if the good God wishes it, you will enter; let the Superiors decide.' That had lasted scarcely two minutes. Next it was my turn. I too had tears in my eyes, and would you believe I had the audacity to say: ' Most Holy Father, a blessing for the Carmel." [1]

"Then he blessed me, while saying: ' Oh! Carmel is already blessed! '

"Papa came quite a distance after us with the gentlemen. Abbé Révérony presented him to the Holy Father, saying: ' This is the father of two Carmelites and a Visitation Nun,' but he did not say he was the father of Thérèse. The Holy Father looked at him particularly, and gave him his hand to kiss and grasped his lovingly."

The manuscript of St. Thérèse adds this detail:

"As a special sign of benevolence the Sovereign Pontiff had placed his hand on

---

[1] My emotion made me forget the principal thing, the word *Lisieux;* it was indeed to the dear monastery I wished to bring back a special blessing.

Papa's head, thus appearing to mark him with a mysterious seal in the name of Christ Himself, whose representative he truly is."

Our Father endeavoured not alone to lighten the grief of Thérèse, but he took active steps again to second her own efforts. He went to pay a visit to a French Religious, the Rev. Brother Simeon of the Brothers of the Christian Schools, Founder and Director of St. Joseph's College. I prefer to quote this passage from my letter of November 23, in which I described this interview to our Carmelite Sisters:

"Let us rejoice! When all seems lost, then all is gained. Papa went to see the Superior of the Brothers to thank him for the kind reception he had given two years ago to Papa and Abbé Marie. The Brother was delighted; Papa spoke to him open-heartedly, telling him of the audience we had on Sunday, the desire of Thérèse, and all the vicissitudes and disappointments which she had endured.

"The Brother learned that Papa's eldest daughter had entered the Carmel also. He had never heard the like of that, and was enthusiastic about our family. . . He took note of all that Papa told him about Thérèse, and he suggested speaking about it to Abbé

Révérony.   But listen to what happened,
Papa rose to leave, when who should enter?
Abbé Révérony! . . .   Imagine the surprise
of Papa and of the Brother!

"The Abbé was charming with Papa, and
seemed to be sorry. . .   Papa then asked him
if there were any reply from the Bishop, and
added: '*You know how you promised to give a
helping hand.*'   What a kind father!   Then he
told about the sorrow of Thérèse at the
audience especially when the Abbé answered
that the question was being examined by
the Superiors, etc.   The Abbé was really
touched, I believe, and he is beginning to
realize that the vocation of Thérèse is
extraordinary.   He even admitted: 'Well,
*I'll assist at her Clothing Ceremony.   I invite
myself.*'   Papa said that he would be very
happy to have him, and they exchanged a
number of complimentary remarks."

I shall not spend more time in regard to the
return journey; but I shall relate only this
pleasant incident of November 29, at Cannes,
just as I wrote it at the time to the Carmel.

"This morning we happened to be together
with Abbé Révérony waiting for an omnibus
to take us to the railway station.   Papa was
beside the Abbé and whispered to him:
'*If you said a word to Thérèse.* . .'   The Abbé
replied by a smile.   Papa repeated: '*You*

know she is still thinking of her little Jesus at Christmas! ' The same smile for a reply. Then the bus came along and we got in. Thérèse and I were behind Papa.

" By a permission of divine Providence Thérèse was beside Abbé Révérony. There were sixteen of us in the vehicle, eight on each side, and packed in like sardines. The Abbé leaned towards Thérèse and said: ' Well, when we reach Lisieux, what shall we do— where shall we go? ' Thérèse looking for an answer only smiled. The Abbé repeated his question. Then Thérèse said: ' I shall go to see my sisters at Carmel.' ' Well,' said the Abbé, *' we'll do all we can, won't we?'* ' *Oh, yes,*' said Thérèse. Abbé Révérony added: ' *I promise you to do all I can.*' Thérèse then exclaimed whole-heartedly: ' *Oh, thank you!* '

" There is the whole story. I have written it just as it happened."

On her return to Lisieux Thérèse anxiously awaited the authorization of the Bishop. At the advice of Pauline who wrote to him on December 16 a letter of reminder, and also to Abbé Révérony recalling his promise to help her. Our good father encouraged her with all the affection of his heart. Daily he used to go with her to the Post Office to look for a reply. To distract her he suggested a new pilgrimage—to Jerusalem; but that would have retarded her; she desired only Carmel.

It was on January 1, 1888, that she learned through Mother Marie de Gonzague of the definite consent of Msgr. Hugonin. But at the suggestion of Sister Agnes of Jesus her entrance was postponed until after Easter because of the Lenten season, and without doubt also to spare the feelings of Abbé Delatroëtte. During those weeks of waiting, my father showed all his affectionate solicitude for Thérèse. He tried to surpass himself in giving her pleasure. She herself has feelingly related the farewell party at Les Buissonnets on Low Sunday, April 8, 1888. " *Papa scarcely said anything, but he looked lovingly at me from time to time.*" The following morning she set out for the last time on the arm of her dearest " King." After Mass he led her to the door of the cloister, and in tears knelt down to bless her.

> " To see this old man giving his child to God," wrote the saint herself, " while she was still in the springtime of life, was a sight to gladden the angels."

On his return home he showed marvellous courage. I wrote so immediately to Carmel, and Sister Marie du Sacré Cœur replied by the following letter:

" My incomparable Father,

" What Céline has just told us is worthy of you! Ah! what a father we have! And as a result I am not surprised that our Lord accepts all his children from this incomparable father.

" Our Lord's Sacred Heart must love him and his with a very special love.

" And how our dearest mother must smile down on you from on high; how she must rejoice to see you steering her beloved barque so well towards Heaven! O best of fathers, what a responsibility for us if we do not become saints; if we would not follow in the footsteps of your generosity! Ah! how gladly will our Lord give you a hundredfold for the ' Lily ' just opening, full of beauty and purity, which you offered to Him to-day."

As a matter of fact the sacrifice was keen for our beloved father. One of his friends said to him:

" Abraham has no lesson to teach you; like him, if God had demanded it, you would have sacrificed to Him your little Queen." He replied instantly: " Yes, but I confess I would have raised my sword slowly, hoping to see the angel and the ram."

Our uncle and tutor, M. Guérin, had already manifested his enthusiasm for the heroic patriarch who, however, had at that time reached only his third holocaust. On October 15, 1886, the date of Marie's entrance to Carmel, M. Guérin wrote:

> " One day the Lord showed me an old fruit tree laden with five beautiful, ripening fruits, and ordered me to transplant it into my garden. I obeyed; and the fruits ripened successively. The Child Jesus, as in days of old during the Flight into Egypt, passed by three times, and made a sign; the old tree bent down lovingly, and each time let fall one of the ripe fruits into the hand of the Divine Child. . . What an admirable spectacle is that of this new Abraham! What simplicity and what faith! We are but pygmies beside this man! "

*   *   *

Our father's offerings were all being made, gradually and completely; and Our Lord allowed none to pass without granting him the occasion of full merit. Although I had definitely decided to let him know that I would always remain faithfully with him, an unexpected event led me to tell him of my vocation to Carmel. I had received on June 15, 1888, special graces of light and strength which made that vocation still dearer to me without however urging me to reveal it to Papa.

The following day I took up to him in the Belvedere a painting which I had just finished representing our Mother of Sorrows and St. Mary Magdalen. He was so pleased with it that he immediately suggested that I be given painting lessons in some Academy in Paris. I felt I had to decline the offer, giving as a reason my desire to become a Carmelite. Thus did I let him know my secret. At this unexpected revelation, my dear father wept with joy, and exclaimed with rapture:

> *Come, Céline, let us go together before the Blessed Sacrament to thank the Lord for all the graces He has granted to our family, and for the honour He has done me in choosing spouses in my home.*

He immediately shared his happiness with his Carmelites.

> "I must tell you, my dear children, how urgently I feel the need of thanking God, and of having you join me in thanking Him; for I feel that, although very humble, our family has the honour of being numbered among the privileged ones of our adorable Creator."

Should we not unite to these fatherly strains those which arose from the heart of our

mother?   That is why I recall here the
expression of praise that Thérèse offered to
our parents when she wrote:

> " The good God gave me a father and a
> mother more worthy of Heaven than of
> earth." [1]

A thought which Father Pichon knowing it
echoed when on seeing us all consecrated to
God he repeated insistently to us : " Children,
all that you are you owe to your parents."
And yet they had longed for even more than
daughters who would be Religious.   That is
why Thérèse was to write:

> " I was told that before my birth my parents
> were hoping that their great desire (to have
> a missionary son) was to be realized.   If they
> had been able to penetrate the future, they
> would have seen that indeed it was through
> me their hopes would be accomplished."

Thérèse was referring to the missionary
priest who had then been given her as a spiritual
brother.   But we are justified now in applying
it in a different and far wider sense!   She was
right when she reminded my father of what

[1] Letter to Abbé Bellizre, July 26, 1897.

he himself loved to repeat: " *The good God is never outdone in generosity.*" In Thérèse, *Patroness of Missions*, our parents possessed their missionary, and if they did not give to the Church the " Great Saint " for whom they had longed, they gave to her, according to the testimony of Saint Pius X, " the greatest Saint of modern times." Their dreams were indeed surpassed.

ILLNESS AND DEATH OF MY FATHER

"God hath tried them and found them worthy of Himself. As gold in the furnace He hath proved them and as a victim of a holocaust He hath received them."—*Wisdom* iii. 5, 6.

The offering of his little "Queen" seemed to be for our father the supreme sacrifice. It was only the beginning. Thérèse made the same remark when in May, 1889, she wrote to one of us:

> "Before my entrance to Carmel our incomparable father said, in giving me to God: I would wish to have something still better to offer to the good God. Jesus has listened to his prayer: . . . *the something better is himself.*"

Sister Marie du Sacré Cœur notes on her part:

> "Very often in thinking of Papa I used to ask myself: What will be the end of his beautiful life? I had a secret presentiment that it would end in suffering; although I was very far from imagining what that suffering would be.
> "But when it did happen, I saw so clearly the value of it all one day during Mass that I would not have wished to exchange it for all the treasures of this world.
> "At that time the story of Job recurred to my memory. I thought that it applied to

us as well as to him. Satan, presenting himself to the Lord, had said to Him: *It is not astonishing if your servant praises you—you heap favours on him! Strike him therefore in his own person, and you will see if he does not curse Your Name.* But the Name of the Lord was not cursed. On the contrary it was blessed, in the midst of the most agonizing trials."

It is a good idea at the beginning of this chapter to recall the vision which Thérèse had had in her childhood. She saw in the distance our father in his great distress, like the holy king David crushed with trials, who " went over the brook Cedron . . . went up by the ascent of Mount Olivet, going up and weeping, walking barefoot, and with his head covered." [1] This is how Pauline, who was a witness of Thérèse's emotion, spoke of it at the Apostolic Process:

> " She might have been about seven years old. My father had been at Alençon for a few days, and my sister Marie and I were up in one of the two attic rooms that looked out on the garden, at the back of Les Buissonnets. Little Thérèse was enjoying the view of the garden from the window in the adjoining room. It was in summer; the sunshine was bright, and it might have been

---

[1] *II Kings* xv. 23, 30.

about two or three o'clock in the afternoon. Quite suddenly we heard our little sister crying in an anguished voice: ' Papa, Papa! ' Marie, seized with fright, said to her: ' *Why are you calling Papa like that?   You know very well that he is in Alençon.* '

" She told us then what she had seen at the further end of the garden: a man walking along the pathway, dressed exactly like Papa, of the same height and with the same walk; but *his head was covered* with a veil, and he was bent over like an old man. She added that this man had disappeared behind the clump of trees which was near there.

" Immediately we all went down to the garden; but not having found the mysterious person we tried in vain to persuade Thérèse that she had seen nothing.

" Later on, in Carmel, some years[1] after Papa's death Sister Marie and Sister Thérèse being together on a ' special recreation ' day, recalled this vision, and understood all of a sudden what it meant. Sister Thérèse of the Child Jesus explains this in her *Autobiography*."

I copy here the very words of the Saint in her manuscript:

" It was really our darling father whom God showed me, bent with age and bearing

---

[1] There is a slight mistake here.   In fact this conversation actually took place a few *months* after our father's death.

on his venerable face and silvery hair the symbol of his terrible trial.

" As the adorable Face of Jesus was veiled during His Passion, so it was fitting that the face of His humble servant should be veiled during the days of his humiliation, in order that it might shine with greater brilliance in Heaven beside his Lord, the eternal Word of God.

" It is from the seat of glory that our dearest father obtained for us this consolation of understanding, that ten years before our trial, the good God had already shown it to us. Even so does a father's love prompt him, both to dwell himself with delight on the treasure he has stored up for his children, and to allow those children to catch a stray glimpse of the glorious future he is preparing for them."

* * *

BEGINNING OF HIS ILLNESS

To summarize the different phases of my father's illness, I have used not simply my own very clear recollections, but also the entries of my personal diary. These, like the Stations of a Way of the Cross are noted down day by day.

In the course of his whole life until then our father had had a robust constitution with

great resistance. Towards 1876, an incident
occurred that forced him for the first time to
have recourse to a doctor. One day, as he
was fishing near Alençon, he was stung behind
the left ear by a poisonous fly. At first it was
but a little black spot which scarcely troubled
him at all. Gradually it began to spread and
to cause anxiety. Several doctors were consulted
at Lisieux and elsewhere. The different and
repeated treatments he had to undergo were
extremely painful, particularly the last ones
in 1888. My poor father then endured a real
martyrdom. He who was so courageous could
do no further work, and simply strode rapidly
through the garden, saying to Léonie and me
in a heart-rending voice: " Oh! children,
pray for me! "

It was diagnosed as an " epithelioma." It
spread gradually until it was as large as the
palm of a hand. This local infection was to
disappear only very slowly towards the last
months of his life. In the family, we were
convinced that the cerebral troubles, of which
I am about to speak, were not unrelated to
this intolerable suffering, since the culminating
point of it, together with some kidney trouble,
coincided with a serious and general weakening
of his health.

The first indications of this general debility
had been manifested the preceding year, when

our father was almost sixty-four. On May 1, 1887, on awakening, he had an attack of paralysis, which affected his whole left side. With his usual energy, he wished nevertheless to go with us as he did every day to the seven o'clock Mass, in order to receive Holy Communion on the opening of the month of May. He spoke rather inarticulately, and painfully dragged his leg. He said to Léonie, Thérèse and me:

> " My poor children, we are as fragile as blossoms on the trees in springtime; in the evening we, like them, seem wonderful; the following morning, an hour's frost withers and shrivels us up."

When our uncle Guérin was told of Papa's condition, he summarily put Papa to bed, and applied a dozen leeches. Apart from some lapses of memory, he recovered sufficiently to take an active interest in the confidences of Thérèse regarding her vocation, and to accompany her in all her different steps. He had two other paralytic strokes in the course of the year. During the month of May, 1888, he went to Alençon, and in his old parish church, which was associated with so many memories for him, he had a particular grace, which he related to his three Carmelites on his return, in a visit to the parlour:

" Children, I have returned from Alençon, where I received in the Church of Notre Dame such signal graces and such consolations that I made this prayer: ' *My God, it is too much! I am too happy; it is not possible to go to Heaven this way. I wish to suffer something for you, and I offered myself. . .*' The word *victim* expired on his lips, writes Thérèse, he did not wish to pronounce it before us, but we understood! "

SUDDEN AGGRAVATION OF HIS ILLNESS

Towards the end of this month of May, after Marie's Veiling Ceremony, at which he assisted, his state of health gave us new anxiety. He began to show signs of more emotionalism, and tears came easily and frequently to his eyes. I must say, in truth, that before his illness I never saw him shedding tears, except when our mother was receiving Extreme Unction. Often, while reading some beautiful passages, or listening to a stirring discourse, his features betrayed emotion, his eyes filled with tears; but that was all. Even on very moving occasions he did not allow himself to be excited, and remained perfectly the master of his feelings.

When he knew definitely about my vocation, after June 16, a sort of fixed idea, stimulated also by his piety, took possession of him little by little. He wished to retire into solitude to live there as a hermit. It is doubtless on that account, that he wanted to put his business affairs in order, and to place all his money in secure stocks, which would provide for the material needs of his children. With that end in view, he made various trips to Paris, but several times it happened, contrary to his habitual punctuality, that he did not return on the appointed day, and we became greatly alarmed.

On one of these occasions, when his absence was prolonged more than usual, we were afraid that he might have been killed, for he carried large sums of money on his person. It was then that our saintly Mother Geneviève,[1] an invalid and blind, urgently summoned my three Carmelite Sisters to her bedside in the infirmary, telling them: " *Nothing has happened to him, and he will return to-morrow. Our Lord has told me so.*" Events justified this prediction.

In the course of a similar alarm, when our father had unexpectedly left for Le Havre, a fire broke out in a house adjoining Les Buissonnets, and completely destroyed it.[2]

---

[1] Mother Geneviève of St. Teresa, O.C.D., the Foundress of the Lisieux Carmel.

[2] Soon after, our father bought the land on which the burned property stood. This narrow strip of land was added to the front garden of Les Buissonnets, upon the advice of Mgr. Lemonnier, the Bishop of Bayeux. The house in question was situated where the large steps are placed now, and the plaque of our Saint is set in the wall. As to the back garden, it has stayed always just as it is to-day, in form and in size.

Léonie was alone in the house with the maid.
The Carmelites heard of it, and Madame Guérin
wrote to them:

> " I beg you to calm all your fears. See in
> the case of this morning's fire how your
> sister was protected. If the fire had broken
> out during the night, nobody knows what
> might have happened. I cannot help believing
> that the good God will never permit a great
> misfortune to take place. He may let things
> go very far, just to test our confidence; but
> He will always intervene in time.
>
> " Good-bye, dearest nieces. I embrace
> you with all my heart."

This situation continued with alternation of
improvement and relapse. Even when confused,
all the thoughts of our good father remained
directed towards God's service, which had been
the centre of his whole life, and his acquired
virtues continued to manifest themselves in
spiritual works of charity. Thus he took a
lively interest in the conversion of sinners, and
in particular that of a cousin by marriage of
M. Guérin, who was then seriously ill. He
recommended to the Carmelites this " big fish,"
as he called him. Pauline replied on July 1st,
with a note, in which one feels that she wishes
to prevent him from performing any penances,
and from worrying about this matter.

> " Do not worry, beloved Father, you have done your part in getting everything underway; it is up to us now to continue—besides, that is our vocation."

The conversion was obtained complete and touching.

During the illness his charity only became more manifest. I wanted to have for myself the brass crucifix which was in his room, not knowing that he had received it from Marie before her entrance into Carmel. He hesitated to give it to me. But one day in September during Mass, as he was reading a prayer of General de Sonis I had handed him, he turned to me and whispered: " I give you my crucifix." In relating this episode in a letter to Mother Marie de Gonzague, I added the following to show how much our father was esteemed in the town:

> " On the street everybody salutes him, and he is referred to as the ' saintly patriarch.'
>
> " This evening Léonie and I were in the Cathedral sacristy to be enrolled in some Association, when the pastor of St. Pierre[1] said to us:
>
> " ' Your Carmelite Sisters are quite happy? ' ' Oh! yes, Canon! ' ' And you should be too for you have an incomparable father. Isn't he good? '

---

[1] Canon Rohée.

> " I was quite thrilled to hear Papa referred to with such respect and veneration.
>
> " You see, dearest Mother, how much our dear father is everywhere loved and appreciated."

However, his state of physical depression was becoming more pronounced; and I referred to it in a letter to Thérèse on July 22nd, 1888.

> " Papa seems to have become so old and so worn. If you saw him every morning kneeling at the altar-rail for Holy Communion! He leans and helps himself along as best he can. It would make you cry! "

I shall not delay to describe the different phases of the affliction; he was aware of them, for he was completely conscious, apart from some lapses of memory. Thus one day he said to his Carmelites: " *Children, do not be afraid for me, for I am a friend of the good God.*" At the height of our anguish we had placed in the Carmel chapel, beneath the picture of the Holy Face, a marble slab, with these words engraved in letters of gold: " Sit Nomen Domini Benedictum. F. M. 1888." [1] This slab is now enshrined behind the Tabernacle of the High-Altar of the Carmel.

---

[1] " Blessed be the Name of the Lord. Martin Family, 1888."

CONSOLING INTERLUDE

Our father's illness caused the Clothing Day of Thérèse to be retarded until January 10, 1889. When it was settled upon he prepared for it by offering numerous presents. He wished his little " Queen " to be gowned royally in a robe of white velvet, trimmed with swansdown and Point d'Alençon. Although on retreat, with the permission of the Prioress, the little fiancée of Jesus sent him a message of gratitude, adding:

> " In order not to disturb the silence of the retreat, one is forbidden to write, but how can one's peace be troubled in writing to a saint? "

Thérèse has told in her manuscript the beauty of the day:

> " The feast was enchanting; the most beautiful and enchanting flower of all was my darling " king." Never was he more beautiful or more noble. He was the admiration of all. That day was his triumph— his last feast here below! "

Papa was waiting for her at the door of the cloister. When she appeared, he pressed her to his heart, and with tears in his eyes, " Ah " he exclaimed, " there she is—my little Queen "

Then giving her his arm, he solemnly entered with her to the adjoining public chapel. We who had seen him so ill could not thank God enough to see him again so courageous. A touching detail: Brother Simeon had obtained for the occasion a special Papal Benediction for him and for Thérèse.

At the end of January Papa went alone to Alençon on some business matters. It was the last time. But this relief did not last long. Thérèse writes in her *Autobiography*, referring to the High-Altar of St. Pierre:

> "Papa had offered an altar to God; he was himself the chosen victim to be immolated with the spotless Lamb."

A little further on she declares:

> "January 10th was Papa's day of triumph. I likened it to the feast of Christ's entrance into Jerusalem on Palm Sunday, for his day of glory was followed by a dolorous passion, just as in the case of Our Divine Master, whose Passion was not for Himself alone. As the agony of Jesus pierced the heart of His holy Mother, so were our hearts deeply wounded by the humiliations and sufferings of him whom we loved best on earth.
>
> "I remember how in the month of June, 1888, when we were afraid Papa might be stricken with cerebral paralysis, I said: '*I am*

suffering a great deal, yet I feel I can suffer still more.' I did not then suspect the cross that awaited us. Neither could I know that on February 12, one month after my Clothing Day, our beloved father would drink so deeply of such a bitter chalice. Ah! that day, I no longer protested that I could suffer more. . ."

IN THE MENTAL HOME IN CAEN

Alas! there were fresh lapses of memory, with new and stronger congestive strokes. Our uncle, M. Guérin, insisted, in the interests of the dear patient himself, that he should be cared for in a Home specializing in such cases. On February 12, a day of grief, which Thérèse called "*our great riches*," our beloved father was placed in the Bon Sauveur Home at Caen. He went there without knowing where he was being taken, but he realized as soon as he entered. His first reaction changed into sentiments of humility and surrender to divine Providence. From his arrival he gained the esteem of everybody, so that Mother Lecoquil, the Assistant General of the Institute, wrote to me:

> " You can be assured that your dear patient, who inspires everyone with a deep veneration, is the object of our most considerate attention."

A week later, February 19, Léonie and I took rooms with the Sisters of St. Vincent de Paul at Caen in order to be nearer him, and to follow his condition from day to day. During our visits, when he was relatively well enough, he used to repeat constantly:

> " I am very well here, and I am here because it is the Will of God. I needed this trial. Besides I can do good around here. How many need conversion! "

The devoted attendants encouraged him by this thought, as I wrote to my Carmelite Sisters a few days later:

> " The Sister said to Papa that he would render a great service by converting those without religion. ' You are an apostle here,' she said to him. ' That may be true,' replied our beloved father, ' but I would prefer to be an apostle elsewhere! However, since it is the Will of God! I believe it is to humble my pride.' If you only knew, dearest Sisters, how that word went to my heart. I find Papa so holy! "

Some time afterwards he made a similar declaration to the doctor:

> " I was always accustomed to command, and here I must obey, it is hard! But I know why

> *God has sent me this trial. I never had any humiliation in my life; I needed one.'* The doctor replied: ' Well! This one can count.' "

The Reverend Mother who was in charge of the section of the Home in which our father stayed was Mother Costard. It was such a comfort to see her thoughtful kindness towards our patient, and on March 4, I told my sisters about it:

> " Mother Costard takes care of Papa, absolutely as if he were her own father. For the short time he has been here, she told me, he has made himself loved by all; besides he has something venerable about him. One can feel that he is the bearer of a mysterious trial."

A little later I wrote:

> " Mother Costard has told me that she does all things for Papa, just as she would for her own father, who is in the same condition, but is cared for at home by his son. She says also it is a grace of God for her, and that she feels as deeply for our beloved father as for her own."

Our father continued to be interested in us, as may be seen from my letter to the Carmelites:

" When Papa sees me, he asks about everybody and thinks of different persons and things. I believe that we shall not be allowed to visit him more than once a week. But we go every day to make inquiries about him.

" Mother Costard, after having referred to other patients said, in speaking of Papa: ' M. Martin is not in that category, he is paralysed.' She finds his speech a bit difficult and his movements are slower; he walks with difficulty."

Or again, in another letter:

" Papa feels that he is not forgotten, knowing that we are staying at Caen to be near him. Every day a Sister reminds him that we are there, and that we call daily to inquire for him. That seems to please him.

" He was very, very pleased with your letters.[1] They did him a lot of good; all day after having read them, he was in better spirits; he seemed to have new courage. They made him see his condition as a trial of a great friend of God, and those thoughts strengthen him. Do write to him often, as often as you can. The least thing helps him; you know how a single thought sometimes is enough to comfort Papa."

---

[1] Those letters have not been preserved.

He remained continually in the same state
of self-surrender to God's Will.   In a letter
of March 15, I explained to my uncle and my
aunt how impressed we were to see that our
father was completely aware of everything
during the visiting hour that we had just spent
with him, and I added:

> " I told Papa that we were all making a
> novena to St. Joseph to ask for his cure and
> return to Lisieux.   To which he replied:
> ' *No, you must not ask that, but only the Will
> of God.*' "

By his example he did good around him.   I
copy from a letter of April 17, the following,
detail, which deeply edified the attendant who
reported it:

> " Mother Costard gave Papa two little
> cakes, but he pushed them away.   Then the
> Sister in charge came and asked him why he
> would not eat them?   Our beloved father
> answered that during Holy Week he did not
> wish to eat these delicacies."

So he realized that we were in Lent, for he
used to follow punctually the ceremonies of
the Church.   When he was well enough, he
went as usual to daily Holy Communion and
assisted at Mass.   The Chaplain and Sisters
assured me of that.

Always mortified and charitable, he never wished to keep for himself alone the little delicacies that we tried to procure for him and he consistently shared them with his neighbours. Did they not see him passing around his dish of oysters, and scarcely keeping any for himself?

On our visit of May 8, Mother Costard explained that since, according to the regulations, we could see Papa only once a week, it would be wiser for us not to stay on at Caen. Besides she promised that she would inform us of the least change. It was hard for Léonie and me, but it was beginning to affect our health, and our uncle, as well as our sisters, prevailed upon us to return to Lisieux, which we did on May 14. Every week we returned to Caen to visit our beloved father.

Although we had rooms with M. Guérin's family, we did not go out much. Still, our uncle wished to take both of us at the beginning of the holidays to La Musse. He had just inherited, along with my aunt's sister, this beautiful property situated about five miles from Evreux, which included, besides the castle on the heights, some eighty acres of woodlands and meadows, entirely enclosed by walls. It was at the time of this two weeks' absence that Mother Costard gave these details to the Mother Prioress of Carmel on the continually detached dispositions of our father.

" We spoke for a long time of all his well-beloved children, and on learning that Mlles. Léonie and Céline were in the country at La Musse he exclaimed: ' *Oh! how lovely! Tell them to stay there as long as their good uncle thinks best. I do not want them to return to Caen on my account. I am well, very well here.*' This venerable patient speaks only of ' the greater glory of God.' He is really admirable. Not only does he never complain, but everything we give him is ' excellent.' It is touching to see the affection of this patriarch for his family.

" At the request of his children I had bought some strawberries and raspberries for him, which pleased him very much; but there are scarcely any more on the market. I do not know what to give him next, for I cannot find out from him what he would like; and in spite of that, when something special is offered to him, he is endless in his expressions of gratitude."

In March, 1890, we began a novena for Papa to the Holy Face. Mother Costard wrote to me in regard to this on the 27th:

" I received your letter yesterday evening, too late for an immediate reply. Your good father is about the same as when you saw him last; but he can not stand on his feet. If you were living in a quiet, remote place, I would advise you to take him with you as he is not difficult to be cared for; and it would be a consolation for him to be living in your midst.

" What urges me to suggest this is that your father does not even try to get up by himself at all now. His legs must be completely paralysed for him not to do that.

" We join with you for the novena, and each day I make a sign of the cross on his forehead with the oil of the Holy Face shrine."

This paralysis of the lower limbs made very slow and irregular progress. This is how I told our Carmelite sisters about our visit of May 20: " In going to the parlour, I met M. Vital Romet[1] and Madame Benoit[2] who were also going to see him. They stopped the carriage, and we got in with them. Our poor father was much touched; he keenly appreciates the visits of his old friends.

" Father was charming. When M. Vital wished to go, saying: ' Now, I must leave you with your children,' father replied with the kindest expression: ' Oh! do stay; you will not be an outsider.'

" They left finally.

" Our Lord had arranged a very consoling day for us. When we arrived he had just

---

[1] One of his Alençon friends.   [2] His sister, married at Caen.

returned from the Month of May devotions, in which there had been a reading on the respect due to old people, and the veneration of white hair. Papa was greatly touched by this.

"At present his legs are becoming numb and it is only with difficulty that he took a walk around the garden with us. At first, while leaning on my arm, he let go of Léonie's. But gradually he was losing control, and he could not have gone on long without falling. He realized that, for he leaned against the wall, saying that he was not tired but that everything was swimming around him. Léonie then gave him her arm.

"The poor dear heart spoke about the three of you, and about Mother Marie de Gonzague, and Mother Geneviève. He was enchanted with your letters. '*I was not able to read them all*,' he said to me, '*because they were too beautiful, and made me weep*.' He did not ask to go away and when I said to him: '*Nothing is long which has an end*,' said he: '*That's true, and I believe we are getting near the end*—it won't be long now. . .' He wanted to talk about his return. He spoke in such a resigned and kindly way! I believe truly that the longer he lives, the more the expression of his face becomes peaceful and holy."

However, the Profession of little Thérèse was approaching. It was definitely scheduled for Monday, September 8, 1890. She had asked me to have our father bless the (copied) formula of her vows, and the crown that she was to wear that day. According to her wish also, I placed the crown on Papa's brow. And finally she solicited from Brother Simeon[1] a Papal Benediction for her " King " as well as for herself.

> " It was a great consolation for me," she wrote, " to obtain for my dearest father the grace he had obtained for me on taking me to Rome."

The Veiling Ceremony was to take place on Wednesday, September 24. Thérèse ardently longed for Papa to assist at the Ceremony and to bless her on the spot. Several times already we had made the necessary arrangements to have him brought back to Lisieux, but the condition of his legs prevented it.[2]

During the summer that year our hopes seemed to be better founded. Our Father was able to go by carriage on the annual outing to the country house of the Bon Sauveur. It was proposed that he could go by train to Lisieux to see his Carmelites. We were planning to

---

[1] Brother Simeon died in 1899 at the age of eighty-five.

[2] He could not be allowed to leave the Home even if he were able to walk, because of the danger of his straying away.

choose the day of Thérèse's taking the Veil. Papa would not have assisted at the Ceremony, but I thought of just getting him at the close, and of taking him quietly to the grille, in order that he might give his blessing to his " Little Queen."

However, our uncle Guérin was absolutely opposed to his coming, fearing the consequences to him of such deep emotions. Thérèse felt the disappointment keenly. It was on that occasion she wrote to me the letter of heartfelt grief on September 23, a letter filled with tears, but at the same time with holy self-surrender:

> " Jesus wishes me to be an orphan. He desires me to be alone with Him alone, in order to be more intimately united with Himself."

Father Pichon, who was also prevented from coming to assist at the Ceremony, wrote to Thérèse from Canada:

> " My Alleluia is mingled with tears. Neither one nor the other of your fathers will be there to offer you to Jesus."

But he encouraged her to offer to Our Lord this " crown of thorns." And in a letter addressed to me he says:

"I drink to the last drop your bitter chalice. The dear patriarch is present in my thoughts at the holy altar and everywhere. Yes, truly he has been chosen as a victim, and that explains everything. Be proud of it, and also grateful to Our Lord."

The following October 1, our cousin Jeanne Guérin was married to Doctor Francis La Néele of Caen, and went with him to live in that town. She kindly invited us to go to see her, and even to remain some weeks, to be nearer our father. It was during one of my trips there that I sent these lines to my sister Léonie, at Lisieux:

"Oh! my dear Léonie, when shall both of us be able to take care of our dearest father? I believe that we would use all our strength and all our love for that. The very thought of it makes my heart beat with joy. The hardships of the task do not frighten me, and I am ready to undergo them till death for him.

"Oh, let us pray very hard that Our Lord may grant our desires, and make the realization possible. But meanwhile let us learn how to suffer and not lose the merit of so many annoyances." [1]

As to Thérèse, she was ever our angel of consolation. Speaking of Jesus, of "His

[1] November 12, 1890.

look veiled with tears," she wrote to me on April 26, 1891:

> " He has taken from us the one we love so tenderly, in a manner even more afflicting than when He took our dearest mother from us in the springtime of our life; but surely He did so that we might be able to say in all truth: *Our Father who art in Heaven.*"

She invited us especially to fix our gaze upon Heaven:

> " Then," she said, " we shall see waves of light issuing from the shining head of our dearest father, and every one of his white hairs will be like a sun pouring joy and happiness upon us." [1]

RETURN TO HIS FAMILY

The exile of our dear father lasted until the month of May, 1892, when, with the complete paralysis of his legs, we were at last able to take care of him ourselves. However, it is remarkable that even in his attacks of nervousness or of sadness, he never showed signs of revolt, nor of any violent or unbecoming behaviour. That explains also what made him seem so touching in the midst of his infirmities and what drew sympathy.

---

[1] July 23, 1891.

It was on Tuesday, May 10, that our uncle, M. Guérin, went to Caen to bring him home. That day my aunt wrote about it to her daughter, Madame La Néele, who was then travelling with her husband.

> "To-day your father went to Caen to fetch your uncle; he brought back dear M. Martin at four o'clock. The journey passed off quite all right. His morale is as good as one can expect; but his poor legs cannot support him any more. He had to be carried to and from the carriage. He wept with joy the whole way, and seems so happy in the midst of his children. He is well settled with us. Céline and Léonie are very happy; they had looked forward to this day for so long!"

During the journey Papa was so touched to see his brother-in-law taking such care of him that, full of gratitude, he said: *In Heaven I'll repay you for all this."* My uncle was quite moved by these words. All the Guérin family helped us to lavish attention upon him, and our aunt, full of veneration for the dear invalid, and for the departed mother whose place she was taking with us, wrote to Thérèse:

> "Your parents, dear Thérèse, are among those who can be called saints, and who merited to bring forth saints."

On May 12, our father was taken to Carmel. It was his last visit as it was feared that too much emotion would harm him. When at the moment of his leaving the Carmelites were saying good-bye to him, he raised his eyes pointed with his finger to Heaven, and remained thus for quite a while, being unable to express his thoughts except by these words, uttered in a voice full of tears: " *In Heaven* ! "

Madame Guérin wrote of the interview to her daughter Jeanne:

> " Your uncle is always as well as we can expect. He spends the afternoons seated in the garden. He recognized distinctly all the members of the family; but it was particularly touching at Carmel. He was taken there on Thursday. You would have thought the day had been chosen, and I truly believe Our Lord had blessed it, for it was the finest day we have had. He seemed to realize everything that took place.
>
> " The Carmelites were so delighted to see their father; but after the first moments, the tears they had held back did flow. They found him quite changed; yet on the other hand, here we find him physically less changed than we had expected. In a word, they are all full of gratitude. It was touching to see the way they expressed it to your father."

In June on the second Sunday of Corpus Christi the Guérin family made an Altar of Repose for the Procession of the Blessed Sacrament. It was arranged in front of the house, and the altar was beside the open door of my uncle's office. All of us used to gather together there, and this year our dearest father was in the centre surrounded by all his family circle as with a crown. When the Archpriest of the Cathedral, Canon Rohée, had given Benediction of the Blessed Sacrament to the crowd, he entered the room and placed the Monstrance on the venerable head of our dearest father. . . Oh! what an acceptable Thabor it was for Our Lord, while tears filled the eyes of the dear invalid.

Some time afterwards, in order that we might be freer, our uncle rented a small house for us at 7, Rue Labbey. It faced our uncle's back garden, of which I had the key, by the tradesmen's entrance. We were very often, if not practically always, in the garden. We used to take Papa there in his little wheel-chair. We had engaged a married couple to help us with the household work.

Father occupied a room on the ground floor, for one could not dream of taking him upstairs. He was as happy as he could be. His manservant, Desiré, had a very cheerful disposition; he was tall, and Papa, whose arms were not paralysed, had only to put one arm around

Desiré's neck to be lifted out of his carriage or to be placed in his armchair. Nevertheless, this moving was always painful for him. His legs remained stiff, incapable of all movement, and he could not stand up.

On the other hand, he took an interest in everything that went on around him; and his last years were relatively happy. He spoke but little, and usually just observed, judging things in a normal way. Thus when he learned of the first election of Mother Agnes of Jesus, his Pauline, as Prioress, February 20, 1893, he exclaimed immediately: " They could not have made a better choice." Another time, having noticed a defect of conduct among my uncle's servants, he did not wish, through delicacy, to tell me about it, but requested me to call his brother-in-law that the latter might correct it immediately.

One day we were speaking in his presence of the wheel-chair which had been loaned to us, and saying that we were hoping to find one for sale. When we actually found one, he expressed his pleasure so strongly that I was very surprised. He had, contrary to what we thought, followed our conversation. On several occasions the same thing happened, and caused us great surprise when we became aware of it. This made us feel that at times our dear invalid could realize his helplessness, and suffered from his inability to express his thoughts and feelings exteriorly; for his soul had never ceased being profound and poetic. . . Thus he loved to listen to the melodies played on the piano by his godchild, Marie Guérin. He would stay there in a kind of rapture for a long time.

In recalling how he continued to practise virtue, even in his absentmindedness and weakness, I think of the words of Jeremias:

> " Blessed be the man that trusteth in the Lord, and the Lord shall be his confidence. And he shall be as a tree that is planted by the waters, that spreadeth out its roots towards moisture; and it shall not fear when the heat cometh . . . neither shall it cease at anv time to bring forth fruit." [1]

On July 26, 1892, I gave this account to Madame La Néele:

> " Papa is fairly well, I cannot say very well, for he has had several very sad days. He seemed to be seized with great anguish and attacks of weeping which tore my own heart. To-day he is cheerful again, and I can breathe freely. Yesterday he kept saying to us: ' Oh, children, do pray for me.'

---

[1] Jer. xvii. 7, 8.

> " Then, he asked me to beg St. Joseph
> *that he might die a saintly death.*"

On June 23, 1893, Léonie went to Caen to make a retreat at the Visitation Convent, with the desire of remaining there, for a new test of her vocation. She did in fact remain there until the death of our father. The preceding year, 1892, when Papa had returned home, it was not considered possible to take him to La Musse, on account of the problems of transportation. A thousand precautions were necessary for the dear invalid, besides transporting his invalid-bed, his wheel-chair, and other luggage. At that time there were no motor-cars, and one had to use either carriages more or less convenient, or the train, to get the invalid there. The property was quite far from the railway station. Even from the gateway lodge there remained almost two miles of winding road to reach the plateau. But for the summer of 1893 my uncle had resolved to try the experiment, which succeeded very well.

> " My uncle is radiant since he arrived here," wrote Marie Guérin to her sister, Madame La Néele. " *He is much happier,* he says, *than at Lisieux.* Céline and I wheel him for excursions through the woods, but

what entertains him best is to look at the beautiful panorama from the heights. A few days ago he just could not cease gazing at it with delight." [1]

I wrote to my sisters on July 3.

"I know how happy you are to receive news of Papa. He is getting on well, but the day I wrote to Mother Marie de Gonzague he was exceptionally well. I had never before seen him like that; and I shall remember all my life the beautiful expression of his countenance, when in the evening, at twilight, we stopped in the depths of the woods, to hear the song of the nightingale. He listened with an awareness in his look! It was like an ecstasy, something I just can't explain—a touch of Heaven reflected on his features. Then after a long moment of silence, while we were still listening, I noticed tears rolling down his cheeks. Oh! what a beautiful experience!

"Since then he has not been so well. That extraordinary consolation could not last; and yet, in spite of all, how happy are his last days. Who could ever have imagined it? The good Lord is treating us with ineffable goodness."

----

[1] June 30.

THE LAST DAYS

On Sunday, May 27, 1894, I was at Caen, staying with my cousin, Madame La Néele, to help her with the Altar of Repose for Corpus Christi, when Papa at Lisieux had a serious stroke, and he received the Last Sacraments.   Doctor de Corniere had been called in.   He hoped that the paralysis, having affected only the left arm, would not go further. As soon as I received the telegram which my uncle had sent, I returned as quickly as possible, begging God to let me be there for the last breath of our well-beloved father.   As a matter of fact, on my arrival he seemed to be recovering again.   On June 5th he had a serious heart-attack.   They came immediately for me at the seven o'clock Mass at the Cathedral of St. Pierre, where I was with my aunt and Marie Guérin.   That same day I told my sisters about it thus:

" This morning again, Papa had a very violent attack while I was at Mass; they came to call me.   It was not a paralytic stroke as before, but a heart seizure.

" My uncle told me that father had a serious heart condition, which would end his days. He considers his condition very critical, although Papa seems to be better this evening. Two hours after the attack one would never have suspected that he had been so ill; and he had been all right when I left to go to Mass. It happened all of a sudden.

"It seems that poor father became purple and that his heart was not beating. My uncle thought that I would not reach home in time. In fact, while running the whole way home, I did not know whether I would find him better or dead. Our Lord wished me not to be deprived of assisting him in his last moments; help me, dearest Sisters, to thank Our Lord for that grace. Oh! pray for both of us. Papa and me! I feel my heart so filled with emotion. Yet this evening Papa seems to be well again; he is resting.

"I do not know when I can go to see you; I am afraid to go out any more. Léonie writes that she is again suffering from eczema on her head, due to wearing the head-dress night and day. I am worried about it."

On June 7, Marie Guérin sent a note to her sister:

"My uncle is having a hard time to recover from his last attack. At times his breathing is very heavy, and at other times he scarcely breathes at all. He appears utterly prostrate, and completely exhausted."

Nevertheless, an improvement allowed us to set out for La Musse on July 5. My aunt writing from there to her mother, Madame Fournet, gives an account of it.

> " I am sending you this morning the latest news. Our journey went very satisfactorily. M. Martin bore it all very well. And if it were not that he is not able to bear as much as last year, and that he is still more helpless, we should have had no difficulty at all. So my husband is very pleased; and La Musse is always so beautiful."

On July 28, our venerable father had another heart-attack, less violent than the last one, but more prolonged. During the evening, Abbé Chillart, the pastor of St. Sebastian,[1] gave him Extreme Unction again. My uncle was absent, having left for Lisieux, to speak at the distribution of prizes at the Brothers' School. He was to return that night. On the 29th, at five o'clock in the morning, Desiré came to call me. Our poor father had his eyes closed, his breathing was strong and regular. Soon after, Desiré, Doctor and Madame La Néele, with some servants, left by carriage for Evreux, in order to assist at an early Mass, and return in time to allow another group to go to St. Sebastian for the eight o'clock Sunday Mass. It was during this first absence that I was

---

[1] The village church.

watching by Papa almost alone. My aunt
came in from time to time to his bedside.
Towards a quarter to eight, we noticed that
my father was icy cold. My aunt left me to
get some hot-water bottles, and to awaken my
uncle who was resting after the exhaustion of
his night journey. I was praying with all my
heart, begging God to inspire me as to what I
ought to do, for I had never assisted a dying
person. Then I said out loud these three
invocations:

"Jesus, Mary, Joseph, I give you my heart,
my soul, and my life.

"Jesus, Mary, Joseph, assist me in my last
agony.

"Jesus, Mary, Joseph, may I breathe forth
my soul in peace with you."

At that moment my beloved father opened
his eyes, fixed them on me with affection and
inexpressible gratitude. His eyes were filled
with life and understanding. And then he
closed them forever.

Almost immediately my aunt returned,
followed by my uncle. The breathing became
suddenly very weak, and quietly like a child
going to sleep his happy soul took flight to
Heaven. It was a quarter past eight. Papa
was seventy-one years old lacking a month.

We were alone my uncle and I at the moment of his death. During his agony my uncle pressed the crucifix several times to his lips, and when he had passed away, I arose and laid my fingers on the closed eyelids of my beloved father. He had such an expression of super-natural joy and serenity that instinctively one thought of St. Joseph on his deathbed. Besides the photograph shows this resemblance. I wrote to my sisters in Carmel:

"Papa is in Heaven. I received his last sigh, and closed his eyes. His fine countenance immediately took on an expression of happiness and profound peace. Serenity is marked on his features. He died quietly at a quarter past eight.

"My poor heart burst at the last moment, and a flood of tears bathed his bed. But underneath I was really glad for his happiness after the terrible martyrdom which he has undergone and which we have shared with him.

"Last night waking up suddenly from an anguished sleep, I saw in the sky something like a luminous globe. And this globe slowly disappeared in the immensity of Heaven.

"To-day we have the Gospel of the five wise virgins. It is Sunday, the Day of the Lord. Papa will remain with us till

August 2, the Feast of Our Lady of the Angels.

Your Céline.

" P.S. We shall probably arrive (at Lisieux) to-morrow.   Last evening Papa received Extreme Unction, Absolution and Plenary Indulgence.   My uncle said he never saw a more peaceful death."

Our father was laid out in an oak coffin lined with lead.   The pastor of St. Sebastian announced his death with much emotion at the Gospel of the Mass, and gave a eulogy of the venerable patriarch.   On Thursday, August 2, the funeral service was held at the Cathedral of St. Pierre in Lisieux.   A large and sympathetic crowd followed the hearse to the cemetery hill.   After so many humiliating trials his burial was in a sense a triumph.

Soon afterwards there was a solemn service in the Carmelite chapel, at which a sympathetic concourse assisted.   We received many touching marks of sympathy.   People noticed especially the appropriateness of the well-known hymns that were played on the harmonium, such as the following:

> O happy souls, who from their youth,
>   Obediently impart
> Their lives, with innocence, to God,
>   Nor lose their peace of heart.

And again, this hymn, which put a note of joy into the sad service:

> Heaven—my home is there,
> From the elect I came,
> Jesus, my Brother's Name,
> Mary, my Mother fair!

The mortuary card that was printed as a memorial reproduced the venerated Holy Face of Tours. There were scriptural texts added, which exemplified his life; then some thoughts of his own, one of his favourite prayers, and finally the appreciation of his friends in regard to his charitableness.

From Quebec, on July 30, Father Pichon sent the following letter to us:

> " Heaven has then charmed away from us the beloved patriarch. Could we dare to weep for his happiness? After such a life he must have been well received on high. I can see him smiling sweetly on us from the eternal shore, where to-morrow we shall rejoin him in the Homeland, in which he has found again those who have been waiting for him so long.
>
> " Behold him, dearest children, behold your beloved father, in the arms of your saintly mother, surrounded by his heavenly family. You must then smile at Jesus, who

has taken him from you only to give him beatitude. I dare say he is now yours more than ever, oh! much, much more yours than during those six long years of Purgatory, when we saw him dead to earth yet not living in Heaven.

"I can't express what sweet emotion filled me yesterday evening when I received the cablegram. I threw myself on my knees to pray for him, the saintly old man, and to invoke him. This morning I celebrated the Holy Sacrifice for his intentions. To-morrow, in offering the Mass of St. Ignatius, which each year I reserve for myself, I shall give up my own intention in his favour. And my chalice will be all for him, as far as I can have authority over it.

"I bless each and all of you, in the name of Our Lord, of the venerable patriarch, and of myself.

A. P."

Thérèse later on was to express in her poem, *What I Used to Love*, my feelings towards my beloved parent and of his consoling death:

> To my dear father, worn and old,
> I gave myself with love untold.
> He was all to me. Joy and home and gold
> Were mine in him; for him my kiss
> My bliss.

We loved the sweet sound of the sea,
The storm, the calm, all things that be.
At eve, the nightingale sang from the tree.
Oh, seemed to us like seraphim
      Its hymn!

But came one day when his sweet eyes
Sought Jesus' cross with glad surprise. . .
And then—my precious, loving father dies!
His last dear glance to me was given;
      Then—Heaven!

Jesus, with hand benign and blest,
Took Céline's treasure to his rest
Where endless joys are evermore possessed,
Placing him near His throne of love
      Above.

In her letter of August 20, 1894, Thérèse again consoles Léonie:

> "Papa's death does not give me the impression of a death, rather one of a true life. I find him again after six years absence; I feel him near me, looking at me, protecting me. . ."

We know how Thérèse invoked the newly elect in the case of my entrance into Carmel, about which there were great difficulties. She explains it all in her manuscript.

"From Heaven, my beloved King, who on earth did not like delays, hastened to arrange everything for Céline. One day, when the difficulties seemed insurmountable, I said: ' *You know, dear Jesus, how earnestly I have desired to know if Papa went straight to Heaven. I do not ask you to speak, just give me a sign. If Sister A. de J. agrees to the entrance of Céline, or at least does not oppose it, that will be your reply that Papa has gone straight to You.'*

"You know, dearest Mother, this Sister thought that three of us were already too many, and consequently did not wish to admit another. But the good God who holds in His hands the hearts of creatures, and inclines them as He wishes, changed the disposition of this Sister. After my thanksgiving, she was the first person I met. She called me amiably, and asked me to go to your room. There she spoke to me of Céline's entrance with tear-filled eyes."

I entered Carmel in fact, on Friday, September 14, 1894. I took the Habit the following February 5. On that occasion the preacher was Canon Ducellier, Dean of Trevieres, ex-assistant of St. Pierre.[1] He had known Papa very well, and in the sermon recalled his memory with veneration—a fact that made Father Pichon

----

[1] Lisieux.

exclaim with joyfulness: " The saintly patriarch glorified after his humiliations! That is one of those strokes of Providence in which the Heart of God is revealed." [1]

* * *

The memory of our father left a lasting fragrance. During the year following his death Marie Guérin sent me two long letters from La Musse, from which I take, here and there, certain passages:

> " As soon as I got out of the carriage, I made my little pilgrimage to my uncle's room, which enshrines so many memories. I went over it all again. . . I was lost in the thought that there—in that room—he had his first vision of God, and had been well received by Him. I imagined that I too would see something heavenly; and my uncle gave me this thought, while reflecting on the particular judgment: *Judge not and you will not be judged*. I left the room, and ever since I have been filled with that thought. It is engraved in my mind.

[1] Father Almire Pichon died in Paris in the odour of sanctity November 15, 1919, aged almost seventy-seven years. In two sojourns he had passed twenty-one years in Canada, and was much appreciated as Director of retreats for priests and religious— of which he conducted over a thousand. He was known as " the apostle of the Sacred Heart."

" I recall also, broken-heartedly, the grief of my dear Céline, whom I could not console. I go over again the scene of her last kiss to him, and in spite of myself my tears flow once more.

" I remember the least incidents of the last days during which we both used to remain beside him.

" Thus my stay here is mingled with joy and sorrow. I seem to hear again, every evening, on the door-steps the sound of the wheel-chair bringing back my good uncle, and I am quite surprised when I lean out of the window not to see anybody.

" What a host of memories! If you only knew! They are sweet in spite of their sadness, because all the events occurred so sweetly that they left a fragrance behind them."

On July 28, the eve of the first anniversary of the departure of our father for the eternal Homeland, she again wrote me these lines:

" I want you to receive to-day a word from your little Marie to show you that I am thinking much about you these days. I do not forget, I assure you, all that happened last year, and my pilgrimages to my uncle's room will become more frequent than ever. As I told you in May, I can never pass by that room without being struck almost unconsciously by a feeling of calm seriousness that recalls the next world and fills my whole soul. That happens to me often and without any foresight—I become as if obsessed: that is the word.

" I do not know why, but this anniversary, which is sad in itself, does not give me that feeling. It is so certain that my uncle entered Heaven that very day, that I rather feel a sense of happiness for his release. How happy he is now, and how well he merited it!

" Oh! I have resolved to ask many graces of him to-morrow, and I am certain that he will obtain them for me on that day. When we recall and have engraved on our minds his beautiful, calm features, so expressive of quiet happiness, it is impossible that the soul should not be filled by it and drawn to love the good God.

" To-morrow, there will be an anniversary Mass at St. Sebastian. It was announced to-day at the Gospel of the High Mass."

* * *

In subsequent years the property of La Musse was sold and resold several times. The first purchaser was Count de la Bourdonnaye, and the Countess transformed the room in which our father had expired into an oratory. Now this fine domain has become a sanatorium for tubercular patients. One of the chief surgeons erected on the esplanade in front of the

Chateau a bust of our venerated father with that of his saintly Benjamin leaning on his heart. This lovely monument is always kept decorated with flowers. One of the doctors of the Institute wrote to us in 1937: " *Thinking of M. Martin, I had the impression that I was entering a house which had been inhabited by a saint.*"

It may be noted also that for the Canonization of St. Thérèse of the Child Jesus a large painting representing her asking permission of our father to enter Carmel was placed on the façade of the bronze door of St. Peter's at Rome. She was thus enveloping him in her own aureole of glory. Our Saint, in recalling the long, crucifying years which we had endured, thus expresses her gratitude: *Be Thou blessed, O Lord, for the years of graces which we have passed in evil days.*" [1] It is to be noted that it was precisely these words, " *Pro annis quibus vidimus mala,*" that Pope Pius XI had engraved on the Pontifical Seal—called " Ruota," which was used for the first time to seal the Bull of Canonization of St. Thérèse of the Child Jesus. Our Lord had inspired his heart with the thought which arose from ours towards the end of our very painful trial. In regard to this *great sorrow*— which remains our *great riches*—I shall let my saintly little sister, with her supernatural

---

[1] Adapted by the Saint from *Psalm* lxxxix. 15.

genius, have the final word. Referring to the Blessing of Leo XIII on the head of our incomparable father, she wrote in her *Autobiography*:

> " *Ah! now that he is in Heaven, this father of four Carmelites, it is no longer the hand of Christ's Vicar which rests on his brow, prophesying his martyrdom: . . . it is the hand of the Spouse of Virgins, the King of Glory, which gives its aureole to the head of His faithful servant, and never again will the divine hand be removed from the head it has crowned with glory.*"

APPENDIX

LETTERS OF M. MARTIN
FOREWORD OF THE CARMEL OF LISIEUX

We have preserved correspondence from Madame Martin, the abundance and the charm of which have contributed greatly in bringing out her engaging personality. M. Martin, on the contrary, did not like to use the pen, except for business letters. He left to his wife, and later on to his daughters, the pleasant duty of giving the household news. When he received from the Carmel one of those communications that found so many echoes in his own soul, he generally replied by gifts, or short notes that he personally delivered at the " turn." The spiritual talks of the " speak-room " took the place for him of lengthy letters.

However, we have gleaned a few letters, which he wrote to Madame Martin or to his daughters. The principal ones date from the journey he took through Central Europe and to Constantinople in 1885. There is also included a message to a friend of his youth, and a fragment of a letter to the same person, in which he announces the entrance of Thérèse into Carmel.

I

In the course of a business journey to Paris to procure orders for the Point d'Alençon lace.

To Madame Martin.—October 8, 1863.

My Dearest,

I cannot get back to Alençon before Monday; the time seems long to me for I want so much to be with you.

Needless to tell you that your letter gave me great pleasure, except that I see by it that you are tiring yourself entirely too much. So I urgently recommend calmness and moderation to you, especially in your work. I have some orders from the Lyons Company. Again I repeat, do not be over-anxious; with God's help, we shall build up a good little business.

I had the happiness of going to Holy Communion at Our Lady of Victories, which is like an earthly paradise. I also lighted a votive-candle for the whole family.

I embrace you all with my whole heart, while awaiting the joy of being with you again. I hope that Marie and Pauline are being very good!

Your husband and true friend who loves you forever.

II

On the eve of a pilgrimage to Our Lady of Chartres, to his daughter Pauline, a boarding pupil at the Visitation Convent of Le Mans.

May, 1873.

My dear Pauline,

Your mother tells me that you want very much to have a letter from me, even if only a few lines, so I wish to please you.

Pray a lot, my dear Pauline, for the success of the pilgrimage to Chartres, in which I am taking part. It will gather together many pilgrims from all over our beloved France, at the feet of the Blessed Virgin Mary, in order to obtain the graces of which our native land has so much need, in order that it may be worthy of its past.

I will pray for you, my Pauline, and your dear Visitation, in that privileged Sanctuary of the Queen of Heaven.

And let me add this: It is well understood that we are all looking forward to seeing our "little Pauline" at the end of the month without fail.[1]

Your father who loves you.

---

[1] Pauline was then alone at Le Mans, as her sister Marie was ill at home at Alençon.

III

Before coming to Lisieux with his family at Les Buissonnets.

Alençon, November 25, 1877.

My dear Children,

To-day, Sunday, being less busy, I hasten to send you a few words. I am eager to be with you,[1] and I am hurrying the women to finish the Point d'Alençon lace, which is still out with a few lace-makers. But I hope that on Thursday we shall have the pleasure of being all reunited, not to be separated again for a long time.

My dear Marie, tell " little Pauline " that her gold shells [2] won't reach her until next Tuesday; I asked for three instead of two. As for the pins, I believe that it will be easier to get them in Lisieux. The moss to which you refer cannot be found at this time of the year, but we shall try to get some later on.

Dear children, pay great attention to all the instructions of your uncle and your good aunt. You know the great sacrifices I have made to let you have the help of their good advice; do

---

[1] They had been settled at Lisieux since November 15.
[2] To be used for the miniature paintings, which were Pauline's great entertainment.

not then allow a single occasion to go by without profiting by it.

You know, my Marie, my " big girl," " my first one," how much I love you. Continue then to devote yourself more and more to your sisters, so that in watching you they may always have before them a good example to imitate.

Tell Léonie that if she continues to be a very good girl I shall certainly give her something which will make her happy for New Year's Day.

Good-bye, dear children. I press you lovingly to my heart which loves you, and I confide you to your saintly mother.

IV

Alençon, November 29, 1877.

My dear Children,

I shall do my best to reach home to-morrow, Friday, about half-past seven in the evening.

Fortunately, I have finished all my business, and I am eager to return to you. Bye-bye then, for the present.

The two notes I have received—from my Marie and my Pauline—have made me very happy, and the commissions you gave me will, I hope, be well discharged.

A thousand good wishes to M. and Madame Guérin and a big kiss for the five of you.

V

To one of the friends of his youth—a native son of his dear Brittany.

Lisieux, 1883.

Dearest Friend,

You see how I hasten to reply to your good letter.

I really want to congratulate you, or rather with you to thank Our Lord with my whole heart, for the great favour which He granted you last December—a date never to be forgotten! It is only later on that that grace will be appreciated at its real worth.[1]

If " God hath blessed the house of Aaron," [2] He has also blessed the house of Nogrix, for the family is " sailing along at top speed." Let us trust that the wind will not change till all have safely reached the port.

Your letter pleased me all the more that I now live mainly on memories. Those old-time reminiscences are so enjoyable that in spite of the trials I have undergone, there are moments when my heart abounds in joy. . .

I must tell you that Thérèse, my little Queen— that is what I call her, for she is a lovely slip

---

[1] His return to the Sacraments.
[2] Allusion to his friend's quotation, *Psalm* cxiii. 13.

of a girl, I assure you—is quite all right.[1] The numerous prayers carried Heaven by storm, and God, who is so good, was willing to give in.

Recently I spoke to you of my five girls, but I forgot to tell you that I have four other children, who are with their saintly mother, where we hope to rejoin them some day. Then I will not have to say any more with Chateaubriand, " Who will give me back my Hélène? " [2] With Hélène are two Josephs and a pretty little Thérèse.

Last Easter I was in Paris with my two older girls. We spent five full days very pleasantly. On March 25th, at Notre Dame, I participated in a splendid love-feast. At least eight thousand went to Holy Communion—all men ! Monseigneur Guibert gave Communion, and Father Monsabre gave a discourse to the congregation.

We had rooms in the Hotel of Catholic Missions, Rue Chomel.

So you had a chance to see our friend Aimé Mathey ! That reminds me of one of my own kind of little jokes which I must tell you.

Once, perhaps about twenty-five years ago, like you I had polished off some little business

---

[1] The letter was written soon after the miraculous cure of Thérèse by the Virgin of the Smile.

[2] An allusion to a poem of Chateaubriand's.

affairs in Paris, when an idea struck me: " Hello, what about a surprise visit to Mathey, and wouldn't it be fun? "

From thought to deed does not take me long. I set off for the railway station, and took the train for Strasburg. When I got there I did what I once did at your place; I pretended to be examining a winder in the display-window of his watchmaker's shop.[1] When I had spun out my joke, I was received with open arms. I gave his little daughter, who was then asleep in her cradle, a toy-rattle in silver; she is now Madame Antonin.

How far away that time is already! And how I would have liked to see those good people return to the fold of the Church! For a person who has the faith it is so sad to see a fine fellow like Mathey, and so many others, jogging along their happy-go-lucky way without bothering about what lies ahead.

And Lange, the dear, simple man, you didn't mention him! How he used to climb our stairs, four steps at a time! Didn't we have good times together?

Have I run on long enough? It is a long time since I had such an opportunity. Am I perhaps getting into my second childhood?

Good-bye, my dear old friend, whom I love

---

[1] M. Martin had perfected his watch-making at M. Mathey's in Strasburg.

as a brother. Give my best good wishes to Madame Nogrix and to your children.

Before leaving France for his journey to Constantinople.

Paris, August 2, 1885.

Very dear Children,

You are indeed very good to have let me set off on this little escapade, and I shall always be grateful to you for it. Besides, if distance separates us a little, my heart will remain always near you. Do not worry in the least about me, and do not be lonesome for me, children!

If however you feel too sad, write to me frankly about it, my Marie, and address your letter to Munich (Bavaria), c/o Post Office, and I'll abandon this good Abbé Marie.

I am forwarding a dozen gold shells; give two to Céline, and two to my little Queen, with a big kiss on both cheeks.

As for yourself, my " big girl," once again have courage and confidence. I assure you that you will not regret having allowed me to go off. So I embrace you very warmly as well as Léonie.

Do not forget to send the eight gold shells to my " fine Pearl " in Carmel.[1]

---

[1] Pauline had entered the Carmel of Lisieux, October 2, 1882, and had received the name of Sister Agnes of Jesus.

All yours in Our Lord.

P.S.   A lot of friendly wishes to your uncle, your aunt and your cousins. I am in a hurry, for I must be at the station at nine o'clock, and I have not much time.

> A thousand kisses to all my own,
> Your father who loves you.

VII

Munich,
> Thursday, August 27, 1885.

Marie, my " big girl,"

I do not want to leave Munich without having given you a sign of life.

We have already visited many beautiful cities. Yesterday we climbed the " Bavaria "; it was curious enough. Imagine a bronze statue of great dimensions, so large that a person can easily sit on its nose. We also saw the museums, which are very beautiful.

I devoured your letter which I still have before me; and I am so grateful to God for having given me such good children. You did right not to show my letter to your uncle, for I believe that this good Abbé Marie is happy to have me with him. We get on very well together; he is most genial and I like him very much.

By the postcard I am sending you, you can see we did not choose the smallest hotel, and also I imagine that it is going to cost us more this time. However, " war is war! "

Express my best thanks to Mother Marie de Gonzague, and tell my " little Pauline " that I think a lot about her. And say the same to Léonie, Céline and Thérèse.

Now I must stop to rejoin my companion. I assure you I would love to have the five of you with me. Without you, I miss the greatest part of my happiness. Meanwhile, continue to pray for me.

Your father who still loves his " big girl " even more now that he is away from her, and who embraces her again and again, as well as the four others of the same nice nest.

Especially, do not worry on my account.

VIII

Vienna,

August 30, 1885.

Dear Marie,

You must have received a letter from Munich, telling you that all was going well, and that I am very pleased with you all. But I am quite surprised that you have not received the shells and my keys. You would do well to make inquiries at the Post Office at Lisieux, for M. Merlier, 211 Rue St. Martin, Paris, must have sent the parcel.

Now, what shall I say next to you? That everything is getting on "as with the late M. Nicolet—getting stronger and stronger." Abbé Marie is always radiant—he is almost tireless. I find it hard to keep up with him.

Yesterday we visited the monastery of St. Norbert, where we could not have been better received. Abbé Marie presented a letter from R. P. Godefroy, whom we had seen at St. James's (Lisieux).

The city is magnificent—with bridges, the like of which I never saw, even in Paris. There are also Carmelites, but they have not such a good menu as we received at the Premonstratensians, for, imagine, we were served a whole pigeon or partridge a-piece, and enormous pieces of hare. Those good Religious have the reputation of being most charitable, and we have truly experienced it.

All the charming letters I received at Vienna gave me immense pleasure. You will please thank Léonie, Céline and Thérèse, and my " fine Pearl " of Carmel very much for me for their Feast-day good wishes.

I imagined I could see you all around me in

the " Belvedere," and my " little Queen " with her sweet, sympathetic voice, warbling her little compliment. I was so touched by it all that I would have liked to be back in Lisieux, but above all to embrace you all as warmly as I love you.

Why didn't you want to accept your aunt's invitation to go to see them at Trouville? It seems to me that you made a mistake. Anyway, do whatever you like.

Take good care of Felicité,[1] and do not forget to give her the wages for the three months.

If you receive any letters for me, open them if you wish, and keep them for me.

Finally, Marie, my " big girl," " my first," continue to lead your little troop the best you can; and be more sensible than your old father, who is already tired enough of all earthly beauties, and who dreams of Heaven, and the infinite. " Vanity of vanities—and all is vanity, except to love God and to serve Him."

> One who loves you all, and carries you in his heart.

---

[1] The maid.

IX

On Board Ship on the Black Sea.

September 7, 1885.

My dear Marie,

You must have received news of us from M. Retout; I am keeping very well, as is Abbé Marie. We have three days more before we reach Constantinople.

The country is magnificent; but so far I am not finding what Fr. Baudry[1] describes as " a corner of heaven left here on earth." It is undoubtedly very beautiful, but I do not entirely share the enthusiasm of my good companion.[2]

Above all, do not be worried about me. If you could write me a few lines, c/o Post Office at Naples, it would please me very much; for I often think of you all, and I repeat to myself: " Oh! if only I could have them with me, how lovely it would be! " But as there is no way of doing this, it casts a shadow around me. However, in a short time, we shall be all reunited, not to be separated again.

Yesterday evening, we met the parish priest of Verna, quite a young priest, who speaks

---

[1] A Religious, a friend of Abbé Marie, who several years previously had taken the same trip.

[2] The Abbé Marie.

eight languages. He received us so graciously that I shall remember all my life the delightful moments we spent with him. I shall tell you all about it later on. How many things I shall have to tell you! But we must wait.

We were not seasick; the sea was calm and majestic, although we were told that it would be very rough.

Tell me in your next letter if you received the parcel from Paris with my keys?

Give my love to my " Pearl," also to Léonie, to my " brave one," Céline, to the " Queen of my heart," and give my best good wishes to all the members of the Guérin family.

Tell my " little Pauline " that I always remember her, and that I should like to be able to send her all the big fish which I can see from our deck leaping about in the Black Sea. How many of them there would be to take the route towards the Carmel of Lisieux!

We are going to sit down to dinner soon, for I see the stewards preparing tables for us quite near me, while I am finishing my scribbling.

Good-bye, beloved, say a *Hail Mary* for us.

X

Constantinople,
September 11, 1885.

My poor " big girl,"

I can see that you are worrying entirely too much about me, for I assure you, as in my other letters, I could not be feeling better.

Your lovely and much wished for letter was handed to me by a Vincentian Father while we were still on the boat-tender before landing. I often think of you all, and recently I had a beautiful dream in which I saw you so clearly that it was almost real. If only I could convey to you all that I feel in admiring the magnificent things which I see around me! Oh! God, how admirable are Your works!

Constantinople is marvellous, and truly compensates for the trouble that it takes to get to see it; but it is so far away! We have just climbed the Galata tower, from which one can get a view of the whole city; it is a spectacle unique in the whole world. We have already seen the Sultan and his three sons, the eldest seems to be about eighteen years old. We also saw the dancing dervishes, poor creatures who really arouse one's pity, with their diabolical ways and gestures.

We are staying with a family, a Madame

Matich, who remembers very well Father
Baudry's visit three years ago.

You tell me that Mother Marie de Gonzague
and all the Sisters are riddling me with prayers
(like shots at a target); I should like in return
for you to bombard them with big boxes of
tunny fish. I beg you to offer them in the best
way you can the expression of my highest
esteem.

A thousand loving wishes to my dear little
" Pearl " who so cleverly removed all the
obstacles or inconveniences to my journey; tell
her that I love her more than ever—if that were
possible.

Also tell good Léonie, who did her best to
soothe you and to coax you to let me go, that
I would like to know what would please her
as a souvenir from Rome.

Tell Céline, " the intrepid one," and my
" Queen of France and Navarre " to let me
know also what they would like best.

In my last letter, I mentioned that I would
love to get the home news at Naples. I hope
that as I am staying a few days more at
Constantinople, you will have time—by writing
immediately—to let me have a word from you
here.

Tell your uncle not to worry at all about the
money-safe. There is nothing to fear, for
nobody knows where it is. So just lock the

door of the closet, keep the key safely, and D.V. everything will be all right.

You did not mention having received the little parcel I sent you from Vienna.

I am seeing so many beautiful things at present that I am inclined to exclaim: " Lord, it is too much; You are too good to me! "

In a few weeks I shall not just be dreaming about you; we shall be reunited again, for as long as God, in His goodness, wishes us to remain together.

I embrace you, dear Marie, Pauline, Léonie, Céline and Thérèse.

You see that I want to please you, for we arrived only this morning, and I am already answering your note. In return, give me the sweetest pleasure you can offer me by writing to me.

Your father who loves his eldest one so much.

XI

Constantinople,
September 16, 1885.

My dear Marie,

I have just a moment and am using it to send you a few lines—while Abbé Marie is taking a walk to Scutari. We are feeling very well; and we are marvellously situated in this private house, recommended by the Vincentian Fathers.

We would have set out to-day for Smyrna, but the boat service is not running at present. We must wait until Thursday or Friday.

What can I say to you now about this beautiful city of Constantinople? I travelled through it in all directions, and the more I see of it, the more I admire it. There are magnificent things to be seen. We visited several Mosques, the most beautiful of which is certainly Sancta Sophia at Stamboul; it was erected by Constantine in 325.

This Basilica was entirely destroyed by fire in 532. Justinian I rebuilt it, and its present form is due to him. He wished this monument to be the most enduring and the most magnificent of all time. The whole empire was impoverished to pay for its restoration.

The Great Bazaar of Constantinople is a most curious affair. This inextricable labyrinth with its streets, lanes, passages and squares forms a city within the city itself. Each street is given up to its own speciality. The Great Bazaar is closed every evening before sunset, and is opened in the morning towards nine o'clock.

On Fridays the Turkish shops are closed; on Saturday it is the turn for the Jews; Sunday is the closing day for Christians.

We visited also the cistern of Asparis. It rests on sixty-four columns, and was constructed under Leo the Great.[1]

---

[1] 440 A.D.

Now, my " first one," my " big girl," my " diamond," let us talk about our own little affairs. I see in re-reading your last letter that you are taking hold finely—one could not wish for better—while I am away. Continue thus, and you'll make me happy. Poor " big girl," how I should like to have you with me during the whole of my fine trip!

Tell my dear "little Pauline " that I often think of her also, and thank God for having given her such a lofty vocation. Thank her from me for her good letter, and do not forget either to present the expression of my humble respect to Mother Marie de Gonzague. We hope to be at Athens next Sunday, and from there we shall go to Naples. There I am sure that I shall have news from you all. Embrace Léonie, Céline and my Queen warmly; alas, it is impossible to do so for my beautiful " Pearl," through the grille. Finally, give many pleasant greetings to your uncle and aunt, also to Jeanne and Marie. And give a friendly pat on the head to Tom, the good, faithful dog. Does he still " weep " for me?

Your father who loves you.

P.S. You did quite right to give the pears. Give, always give, and make people happy.

XII

Naples,
          September 25, 1885.

My dear " big girl,"

I have just spent a very fine forenoon. I visited many magnificent churches; and all of them are filled with superb mosaics; all very beautiful and very rich.

Naples is an enchanting city, but a person is annoyed there by all kinds of beggars. Even the flies there cling like beggars, and become a mild persecution. But we are feeling well, and I see with gratitude how God continues to pour out His mercies upon us.

Yesterday we visited Pompeii—it is very interesting; later on I'll explain it in detail.

. . . Excuse me, I have to go with Abbé Marie; and I am writing these lines to you in a great hurry. It is only to please you and show you that we are alive. You must realize that! Soon, when we get to Rome, I shall write you a longer letter.

Now, dear girls, be always my joy and my consolation on earth, and continue to serve the Lord well; He is so great and admirable in His works!

Good-bye again, dear children, a thousand thanks for the good prayers that are offered up for the travellers.

Abbé Marie is standing over me, and I simply must stop.

I embrace you with all my heart.

XIII

Rome,
Sunday, September 27, 1885.

My dear Marie,

Here we are at last in Rome, at 6.30 in the morning. St. Peter's for me is the most beautiful thing in the world. I prayed there for you whom I love so much; it is so lovely to pray there!

But how sad to think that the Holy Father is, as it were, in captivity there. That is a blot, and that shadow saddens one in spite of all.

Abbé Marie was quite touched by the little note from Carmel, mentioned by my " fine Pearl " in her letter to me. What a consolation I feel when I see that she is so completely happy, and that Jesus, even here below, is so near to her, and visits her as only He knows how! Let us be grateful to God, my " big girl," and beg Him with all our hearts that He may pour out His graces also on our poor, dear Léonie.

Tell Céline and my little Queen that I think about them very often, and that, if you are pleased with them I shall reward them.

I went to the Post Office with Abbé Marie, and there was nothing for us. Abbé Marie was rather disappointed, for he was expecting at least a letter from his pastor. As we hope to be in Milan Tuesday of next week, write me the news there, if you can. I shall be very glad to hear, too, if you received my two letters from Constantinople.

I am in a hurry for the good Abbé is coming soon to take me with him again to see all the beauties of Rome. It is certainly here that I feel the greatest pleasure. Tell my " fine Pearl " that I am too happy, and that "I offer my back for the burden," for this cannot last. How I rejoice that I shall see her soon again!

As for yourself, my dear " big girl," I am anticipating the joy of kissing you on both cheeks—I mean with a resounding kiss—for I love you so! A kiss also to Léonie, to Céline, and to my little Queen.

Your father who is very, very fond of you.

P.S. After lunch, we have planned to visit the Catacombs of St. Agnes. I surrender you

all to the grace of God, and I pray for you
every day at St. Peter's. The thought of your
mother follows me also, constantly.

It will be soon now . . . very soon!

XIV

Milan,

October 6, 1885.

My dear " big girl " and " first one,"

I am writing to you in haste, for we are about
to leave and, the Abbé is hurrying me.

I received your dear letter, and also one from
my "Pearl." They have given me such pleasure.
I needed it for in leaving Rome I was " like a
one-eyed black cat purring away in a corner
of the fence on a wet day."

I am wondering when shall I reach home?
I hope it will be Saturday evening at 9.30.
But you can plan that I shall return by Alençon,
for I must go there next Tuesday.

I thought of you in all the sanctuaries that
we visited; but there was no possibility of
seeing the Holy Father. I will tell you all
about that.

All that I see is splendid, but it is always an
earthly beauty, and our heart is satisfied with
nothing until it be filled with infinite beauty,
which is God Himself.

Soon we shall have the intimate joy of the family, for that is the beauty which more truly brings us closer to God.

I embrace the five of you with my whole heart.

Your father who loves you.

XV

1888.

To his Carmelite Daughters:

I must tell you, my dear children, how urgently I feel the need of thanking God, and having you join me in thanking Him; for I feel that our family (though very humble) has the honour to be numbered among the privileged ones of our adorable Creator.

XVI

April 10, 1888.

To the Nogrix family:

. . . Thérèse, my little Queen, entered Carmel yesterday!

God alone can exact such a sacrifice; but He helps me so mightily, that in the midst of my tears my heart overflows with joy.

One who loves you,

Louis Martin.

PRAYER OF THE CHILD OF A SAINT

Remember thou how once upon this earth
   Thy joy was found in caring for us all!
Hear now the prayer of those who owe their birth
   To thee, dear father: bless us when we call!
A little while ago in Heaven, our home above,
Thou to our mother's side hast come with saintly
    love.

        Together now ye reign
        In Heaven made one again.
          O'er us keep guard!

Remember thy first-born, thy bright Marie,
   She who was dearest ever in thy sight;
Remember how her charm, her gaiety,
   Her love, her goodness, filled thee with delight,
That daily source of joy thou didst renounce—for
    God;
And thou didst bless the hand, that made thee feel
    His rod.

        Thy " diamond " bright and fair,
        Thy rarest of the rare,
          Remember thou!

Remember thou thy beautiful " pure pearl,"
   The timid lamb once to thy tendence given!
Trusting in God, behold thy lovely girl
   Guide Carmel's flock along the road to Heaven.
Of thy beloved ones, " Mother " is she to-day:
Then come to guide even now thy darling on her way!
        This Carmel of Thine own
        Remember at Heaven's throne—
          Remember thou!

Remember now thy strong and ardent prayer
  Made here for thy third child, thy Léonie!
God heard thee; for to her this earth so fair
  But banishment and exile seems to be.
She too from this gay world to God would turn
    aside;
She loves Him only, and becomes His bride.
       Her ardent, burning sighs,
       Her Heaven-sent ecstasies,
        Remember thou!

Remember thou thy faithful child, Céline,
  Who was to thee like angel from the skies,
When close to thine the Face of Christ was seen,
  Testing thy virtue by great sacrifice!
In Heaven thou reignest now; her task is past and
    gone;
Now unto Jesus Christ she gives her life alone.
       Protect her future days,
       Who very often says:
        Rememberest thou!

And oh! remember thou thy " little queen "—
  The tender love with which her heart o'er-flowed;
Remember where at first her steps have been,
  And whose hand guided her along her road.
Papa, remember now, that in her infancy
Her innocence was given into God's care by thee.
       Even her curling hair
       To thee was dear and fair!
        Remember thou!

Remember thou that on the terrace green
  Her place was often on thy saintly knees;
And murmuring a prayer for her, " thy queen,"
  Thou didst sing softly on the Sunday breeze,
And she upon thy heart saw in thy holy face
A shining of Heaven's light, a strange unearthly grace.
        The beauty, sung by thee,
        Was of eternity!
        Remember thou!

Remember now that Sunday ever blest,
  When thou a pure white flower to her didst give,
And to thy child, close to thy bosom pressed,
  Didst grant the grace on Carmel's hill to live.
Oh, father dear, recall that in her trial-hour
Sincerest proofs were given of all thy loving power,
        At Bayeux and at Rome
        Showing her Heaven as home!
        Remember thou!

Remember that the Holy Father's hand
  Within the Vatican was laid on thee.
The mystery then thou couldst not understand,
  The mystic sign of suffering to be.
But now thy children here to thee uplift their prayer;
They bless thy bitter cross, that won thy coronet
        Upon thy brow—fair sight!—
        There shine, in Heaven's own light,
        Nine lilies bright!

                              August 1894.

Prayers to ask for the glorification of the father and mother of St. Thérèse of the Child Jesus, and for graces through their intercession.

O Lord Jesus, who didst make of Thy servant Louis Martin a model husband and father, grant, we beseech Thee, to glorify him who, by his fidelity to Thy laws, his generosity in offering all his children, and his admirable resignation in trials, merited to give the Church St. Thérèse of the Child Jesus.

In Thy goodness, deign to make known Thy designs in his regard, by granting us, through him, the graces for which we ask. Amen.

O God, our Father, who glorified the humble Thérèse for her abandonment and filial confidence in You, grant our request that her mother, Zélie Martin, may be proposed by the Church as an example of these same virtues, which she practised with such a spirit of faith, in the duties and trials of family life.

Grant also, by heavenly favours, to manifest her favourable influence with You. Amen.

Persons who receive favours by the intercession of Louis Martin and Zélie Martin are requested to make them known to the Carmel of Lisieux, Calvados, France.

Imprimatur ✠ François-Marie,

Bishop of Bayeux and Lisieux,

February 12, 1954.

More Great Books on St. Thérèse! . . .

THE STORY OF A SOUL
The Autobiography of St. Thérèse of Lisieux

Edited by Mother Agnes of Jesus
Translated by Fr. Michael Day

No. 1384. 220 Pp.
PB. Imprimatur.
9.00

Written under obedience, this book conveys St. Thérèse's secrets of great holiness achieved in ordinary life, teaching the "Little Way of Spiritual Childhood"—her "elevator" to Heaven. This method has since been approved and promulgated by Pope Pius XI as a way of holiness for all. Again and again, St. Thérèse shows us how her "Little Way of love and confidence" comes straight from Sacred Scripture. One of the all-time favorite Catholic books!

MY SISTER ST. THÉRÈSE

By Sister Genevieve of the Holy Face
(Celine Martin)

A little classic that is like a second *Story of a Soul*. Conversations, anecdotes of St. Thérèse, her teachings, hidden virtues, amusing remarks, beautiful death—recorded by Celine in the convent. Shows the "Little Way" in practice in Thérèse's daily life. A providential book!

No. 1522. 249 Pp.
PB. Imprimatur.
10.00

Set of both books above. No. 1385.   15.00

Prices subject to change.

More Great Books on St. Thérèse! . . .

THE MOTHER
OF THE
LITTLE FLOWER
Zélie Martin (1831-1877)

By Celine Martin
(St. Thérèse's Sister)

No. 1970. 123 Pp.
PB. Imprimatur.

7.50

An authentic and inspiring look at this great woman who married at 27, bore 9 children (4 of whom died in childhood), ran a home business and is the mother of "the greatest saint of modern times." Zélie Martin is now *Venerable*. Great!

THE FATHER
OF THE
LITTLE FLOWER
Louis Martin (1823-1894)

By Celine Martin
(St. Thérèse's Sister)

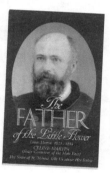

Authentic reminiscences of Louis Martin as a husband, father, business-man, etc., plus the sufferings of his old age and his holy death. Louis Martin is now *Venerable*. Great!

No. 1971. 153 Pp.
PB. Imprimatur.

7.50

Children's Books on St. Thérèse . . .

THE LITTLE FLOWER

By Mary Fabyan Windeatt

No. 1139. 167 Pp.
PB. Imprimatur.

11.00

The Story of St. Thérèse of the Child Jesus, for young people ages 10-100, and of her "Little Way of Spiritual Childhood," whereby she would say "Yes" to whatever Our Lord asked of her, and how she thereby became a great Saint.

CATHOLIC CHILDREN'S TREASURE BOX. *Stories, Poems, Games, Fun Things to Make and Do.* Books 1-10. Ages 3-8. Maryknoll Sisters (1950's). Wonderful full-color series combining fun, innocence and Catholic faith! These books teach children to love God and their holy Catholic Faith and show them how to be good! <u>Stories include "A Little Girl Named Thérèse" (St. Thérèse) in Books 1-6,</u> Wupsy (a Guardian Angel), "The Boy Who Told Lies," etc. For a wide range of ages (Pre-School thru about 10). Children love them! Beautiful pictures!

32 Pp. each. PB. Imprimatur.
10¼" x 8¼". Full color on every page.

(5.00 each.) Set of books 1-10. No. 1371.   40.00

Prices subject to change.

If you have enjoyed this book, consider making your next selection from among the following . . .

Prices subject to change.

Prices subject to change.

Prices subject to change.

Prices subject to change.

The Cause for Louis and Zélie Martin

(*Adapted from the website of the Sanctuary of Lisieux.*)

On March 26, 1994, Pope John Paul II declared Louis and Zélie (Guérin) Martin "Venerable," recognizing their "heroic virtue." The processes for the Canonization of the Servants of God, Louis and Zélie Martin, the parents of St. Thérèse of the Child Jesus, were instigated separately by the dioceses of Bayeux-Lisieux and Sées, between 1957 and 1960. The Causes were then forwarded to Rome. These two Causes are being investigated according to a historical method and are to be presented to the Congregation for the Causes of Saints as one single study or *positio* and will be discussed at the same time. If the Church so decides, this couple will then be glorified together. The faithful are invited to jointly invoke Louis and Zélie Martin to request favors and miracles through their intercession.

Anyone who has received graces through the intercession of Louis and Zélie Martin, or anybody wishing to make a donation or seek information, is invited to contact:

Postulator General of the
Discalced Carmelites
Corso d'Italia, 38
00198 Roma, Italy